At Home in a Big Little World

Rasil Basu

ISBN: 9781720084778

Cover image: Painting by Mary Helen Grace of my home in Delhi
Cover design: Sonali Gulati
Book layout: Michelle Lovi

ACKNOWLEDGMENTS

So many people have built the homes I've inhabited. My first and greatest debt is to my parents, aunt and uncle, whose love, caring, support, and ethical values have influenced everything I've done. I can't think of anyone who made me laugh as hard or care as much about Sikhism and the Punjab as my brother Patwant. I am grateful to Romen for the homes we created together over the sixty years we were married. His love of poetry, food, writing, and travel was contagious. The title of this memoir is inspired by his poetry book, *Big Little World*. Tragically we lost Rob unexpectedly early; I dearly miss his warmth, ready wit and charm. I also mourn the loss of Mark's sister Judy.

Without the support of some generous friends, I would have been unable to pursue the many projects I've undertaken. I am grateful to Kanval Dhillon, Satjiv Chahil, Laurel Marx, Geoff and Diane Ward, Richard Lapchick, Inderjit Singh Jaijee, Ghazala Khan, Deidi Von Shawen, and especially Jean Beard. I am unable to name all my loving and devoted friends but please know much I appreciate all of you.

And then there are the people who encouraged, nagged, and inspired me to write these memoirs. Carol Guensburg and Julie Gammack provided useful suggestions. Meher Wilshaw, Robyn Brentano, and Pat Jones typed up portions and kept track of numerous drafts. Renee Schultz flew to Delhi to work with me and kept track of my progress thereafter. I cannot adequately thank Pamela Philipose, who encouraged me to tell her my stories and then seamlessly integrated them into the draft. Mary Helen

Rasil Basu

Grace took many of the photographs for this book. She also did two beautiful watercolors of my home in Delhi; one appears in the interior and the other on the cover. Sonali Gulati pulled all-nighters researching topics I discuss, designing the cover, and meticulously editing the photographs and the text; this memoir is far more attractive and readable as a result of her efforts. Thanks also to Michelle Lovi for her expert production of the book. Rekha, Amrita, and Mark worked ceaselessly on the manuscript. I cannot adequately thank them.

TABLE OF CONTENTS

one

MY CHILDHOOD HOME

I write this memoir as an exploration, an opportunity to reflect on my past and to understand why I became the person I am today. I decided to write as an act of remembrance, of the small and large events that shaped my life, and to revisit memories, both painful and precious. In writing I have relived some moments that are firmly entrenched in my mind while other memories emerged as I put pen to paper. I write this memoir to explore for myself questions I'm often asked: Why did I refuse to have an arranged marriage and insist on a higher education and demanding career? How did I juggle parenting and professional life? Why did I leave my childhood home in New Delhi to live in New York, and then return to Delhi almost forty years later? Where was home?

While answers to some of these questions will, I hope, emerge over the course of these pages, what I do know is that for me, the personal, political and professional were always deeply intertwined. I was a product of the exhilarating experience of the struggle for national freedom—which was inseparable for me from my own quest for freedom. My feminism was inspired by the strong women who raised me and by the strong female role models that blazed a path before me. But my feminism was also born of the constraints, injustices, and inequities I encountered at each stage of my life. In short, my identity was shaped by the confluence of privilege and privation.

* * *

I was born into a Sikh family on October 11, 1923, in Chaklala, a small British cantonment town near Rawalpindi, where my father, Manohar Singh (Papaji to us), was working. Rawalpindi is nine kilometers from Islamabad, Pakistan's present capital. It was in the Punjab, at that time a part of undivided India, a colony of the United Kingdom.

My paternal grandfather, Ishwar Singh, was a merchant in Rawalpindi. His son, my father, Papaji, was born in Rawalpindi. He studied law in Lahore but he and his brother, Trilok Singh, became building contractors. His family arranged his marriage in 1922 to my mother, Gyan Kaur, ("Mamaji" to us), who was born in Amritsar. My father had four sisters and two brothers so there were seven siblings altogether.

Ishwar Singh, my paternal grandfather

Veeranwali, my paternal grandmother

Mamaji came from a distinguished family from Amritsar, the holy city of the Sikhs in western Punjab. Whereas my father's family was middle class, my mother's family were wealthy, educated, landowners. My maternal grandfather was a district and sessions judge under the British. Her brother, my uncle, Harnam Singh, lived in England for a spell. Although trained in law, he never became a practicing lawyer, preferring instead to lead the life of both a privileged gentleman and a political rebel. I recall with pride the contributions my family made to the fields of art, literature, and architecture.

Mamaji

3

*Left to Right: My uncle Harnam Singh, Amrita, and friends,
at our Amrita Sher-Gil Marg home*

My mother's older cousin, Veer Singh, was a poet-intellectual and Sikh theologian, who later came to be recognized as a key player in a movement for the revival of the Sikh literary tradition. The Sikhs conferred on him the honorific term *bhai* to reflect his piety and religious learning. He wrote over 70 books on a wide variety of subjects—from the conditions of the oppressed to the tenets of the Sikh faith. As children we literally worshipped him. His books still line my shelves.

My aunt, Harnam Kaur ("Maaji" to us), who was a decade older than my mother, proved to be a great influence on her life and ours. Maaji had been married young and had many responsibilities but she always ensured that my mother was well looked after. She was the reason, I am sure, that my mother was educated in a convent school and later graduated from Lahore College for Women University with a major in Punjabi literature. In later life, Mamaji remained interested in reciting poems, reading books and telling us tales related to the Sikh gurus.

I grew up in a matriarchal family. Papaji, contrary to existing tradition, developed a very close relationship with his in-laws and came to live and work with them. He looked up to my uncle, Ram Singh Kabli ("Kabliji" to us), who was one of a small number of prominent Sikh contractors. That list included their close friends Sobha Singh and Baisakha Singh, who built the most beautiful houses in New Delhi. Papaji moved to Delhi in 1924 to work with Kabliji in construction. Our family and Maaji and Papaji lived for many years on the same street, adjoining Jantar Mantar. Years later, Kabliji bought a home on Amrita Sher-Gil Marg where my parents, Maaji, my brother Patwant and I lived with my maternal grandmother, and my uncles, Harnam Singh and Kabliji. This has remained my principal residence, many decades later. I'm deeply attached to it.

Papaji was an easygoing, gregarious and kind person. However, he had less of an influence on my daily life than my mother's side of the family because his work frequently took him away from home. Neither Harnam Singh nor Maaji had any children so they treated me and my brother, Patwant, who was eighteen months younger than me, as their own, and showered us with love and attention. All my relatives took a keen interest in my education and gave me a strong sense of ethics and social responsibility. Mamaji's love of literature influenced my passion for reading. Harnam Singh was active in the Ghadar Party, a radical organization that diasporic Punjabis formed to gain Indian independence from Great Britain. His political radicalism inspired me. My other uncle, Kabliji, instilled in me a love of history and nature. I remember memorizing the names of innumerable flowers and trees to impress him. Since he was a diabetic and could not put sugar in his tea, I kept him company by giving up all sweets myself. I took special pride in knowing that I was Kabliji's favorite.

I was deeply attached to Kabliji and Maaji and could not bear to be separated from them. At an early age—perhaps as a five- or six-year-old—I accompanied them on a trip to south India. Kabliji, who had acquired a national reputation for his success as a contractor, was supervising the construction of a railway line in the south. We traveled in covered bullock carts during daylight and slept in them at night. On one occasion, as our covered wagons were parked on the banks of a stream, the villagers informed us in hushed tones that tigers drank water from the stream after dark. We were told to be very still and quiet so that they would not suspect our presence. My lifelong love for travel and adventure probably began at that point.

I have another powerful memory, of traveling with Maaji and Kabliji when I was around nine years of age. They were leaving for Bombay and my parents took me to the Delhi railway station to see them off. So keen was I to accompany them that I threw a loud tantrum. When Mamaji tried to dissuade me, I cried my heart out and soon found myself in a moving train with a doting aunt and uncle. It proved to be a great vacation for me. Not only did I take in the sounds and sights of a city that I was to revisit in the future, I received the undivided love and attention of this beloved couple as well.

Patwant and I had an intense and tempestuous relationship. We fought and competed ceaselessly but also adored each other and spent much of our free time together. Our school was an easy bike ride from home. The wide avenues and roads of that time hardly saw any vehicular movement. Traffic jams were unheard of, and it was perfectly safe to bicycle to school without fear of harassment or accidents.

We lived in an extended family which included Daljit, Papa-ji's son from his first marriage. Daljit's mother had died when he was very young and he divided his time between our house-hold and that of his maternal grandparents. Daljit, Patwant and I got along very well. There were often four other children in our household, two of whom we were especially close to—Adarsh, who was a week younger than me, and Simran, who was Patwant's age. Kabliji and Maaji virtually adopted Chattar, the mother of these children. They met Chattar when she was a young girl and she became deeply attached to them. Chattar stayed with them for long periods of time and since her family came from mod-est means, Kabliji arranged for Chattar to study abroad and later arranged her marriage to Gurcharan. When Gurcharan became interested in pottery, Kabliji sponsored his travels to Japan, Korea and England to meet with talented potters. Kabliji subsequently purchased land for Gurcharan at 1 Factory Road to create what became the famous Delhi Blue Pottery. Gurcharan was awarded a Padmashree, one of the highest civilian awards, by the Indian government. As children, Patwant and I spent hours making pot-tery under his guidance.

We had our share of escapades. Our home in those days shared a boundary wall with Jantar Mantar, a beautifully landscaped 18th century observatory that lies in the center of what is now New Delhi. On hot summer afternoons, when we were supposed to be napping, we would jump over the wall and go there to play. A more fun place for children to explore could not be imagined, with the steps and slats of ancient astronomical buildings provid-ing the ideal recreational environment for frisky children looking to climb and jump. Patwant and the older children had no prob-lem scaling the wall to reach this paradise but I needed help and remember their calling me a sissy.

Unlike most families at that time, my family did not display any partiality to their son over their daughter. They treated me with as much affection and caring as my brother. I enjoyed school and studies, took part in sports, and formed deep friendships. Mamaji was keen that I should also learn cooking and sewing, the "feminine skills" considered essential in those days. But the great love of my life was academics, and I made sure to study hard.

Every winter vacation Mamaji, Maaji, Patwant, and I would visit our maternal grandmother and uncle in their family home in Amritsar. Some of my fondest memories are around rituals of religious observances. I remember particularly a horse-drawn carriage, with its coachman standing in front of their two-storied house, waiting to take us in the early hours of dawn to Sri Harmandir Sahib, which means God's Temple or everyone's temple. It is also known as the Golden Temple because its dome is gilded in gold leaf. For the Sikhs, the Golden Temple holds special significance because it is their seat of religious authority.

I remember as a child waking up very early in the morning to get to the Golden Temple in time to see a ritual performed at dawn: the *granthis* (those who read from the holy book) carried the Guru Granth Sahib (the holy book) from the Akal Takht, a four-story building across a human-made *sarovar*, or lake, along a crossway to the Harmandir Sahib. The rising sun and the outlines of the Golden Temple were reflected in the *sarovar* surrounding the Harmandir, the sanctum sanctorum, the outer edge of which had a broad marble walkway ringed by several historic buildings. Worshippers circumambulated the Golden Temple and *sarovar* throughout the day, sometimes immersing themselves in its water.

From early childhood I learned some of the teachings of the Sikh gurus and philosophers that were compiled into the Guru Granth Sahib. Written in the Gurumukhi language (the Sikh script), it contains 5,894 hymns (*shabads*) written in 60 melodies (*ragas*) by 35 authors, including 6 Sikh gurus. The *granthis* not only read out passages from the Guru Granth Sahib but also interpret them. They read from the holy book on a daily basis in the large Sikh *gurdwaras* (Sikh temples) and also on special ritual occasions in the *gurdwara* we created in our home.

The Sikhs lavish abundant love and attention on the Holy Book, which is often printed in gold letters, and beautifully bound and covered. It is opened early in the morning on a raised platform covered with beautiful silk fabric edged in gold embroidery. For me, this always was—and still is—a truly magical moment when the verses from the Guru Granth, which are set to music, are sung by musicians to the accompaniment of the harmonium and *tabla*. At the end of the kirtan, the concluding prayer, I especially loved the moment when everyone bowed their heads to the ground and were served *prasad,* an offering made of wheat, sugar, ghee and water which is freshly cooked for the morning ritual.

I respected the egalitarianism of the Sikh community. For example, every *gurdwara* includes a kitchen and an adjoining hall where *langar,* the sacramental meal, is prepared and served to all free of charge. Everyone sits together on the floor of a hall which is covered with matting or carpets. Attendants distribute freshly-made bread, *daal* (lentils), and a vegetable on brass or steel plates. All of those who visit are welcomed to the *gurdwara* dining hall, regardless of their religion, caste or class, because Sikhs consider everyone equal in God's temple and kitchen. People can offer donations of food or cash and contribute to the preparing, serving and cleaning required for this communal dining. I also loved the Sikh commitment to *seva* (community service). It led Kabliji and Maaji to create a family trust and Patwant and me to engage in community work. To this day I find the Sikh commitment to egalitarianism and service very inspiring.

Throughout my life I have been a devout Sikh, despite my many secular values. I don't know many prayers, but during stressful times or moments of contemplation, I recite the verses I remember and they calm me and provide solace. I see no tension between my Sikh identity and my aversion to religious sectarianism. In fact, the Sikhism I embrace promotes inclusion. As a child, my circle of friends included girls from various backgrounds: Hindu, Sikh, Muslim, and Christian. Some of them had brothers and it was quite acceptable for all of us to play together. One of my closest friends in school was a Muslim girl named Nafisa Quereshi. We were constantly in and out of each other's home and celebrated all the religious festivals together with great zeal.

Since Papaji was in the construction business, we sometimes had to move to locations where he had building contracts. This meant that we were exposed from a very early age to the ways of life, food, and social mores of other communities and people. Our travels to Bihar, Punjab and south India broadened our outlook and widened our horizons from an early age.

I always had a strong sense of Indian identity. Although I never felt the full weight of imperialism, I was aware of a foreign presence and the dominant role it played in our daily lives. I became especially aware of this during the five years that I spent at the Convent of Jesus and Mary. We studied British and European history but were totally unaware that other Asian, African, and Latin American countries had any history worth studying. The only language of instruction was English.

The first period on a school day was a visit to the chapel followed by a class on religion, which was only about Christianity. The compulsory visit to the chapel, the morning class on religion, and the westernized school uniform, which consisted of a white shirt teamed with a navy-blue tunic, red tie, white socks with black shoes, only underscored the British imperial influence. I was also aware of the school's puritanism. For example, we were not allowed patent leather shoes because they would reflect girls' panties under their skirts.

The convent was run by very strict Irish nuns. I remember being rapped on my knuckles and asked to leave the badminton court one day because I had said the word "gosh" upon losing the game. "You will not take the Lord's name in vain," pronounced a furious Mother Ursula, one of our teachers. Another memory involved what occurred the day that King George V died. On learning of his passing, I happily told my friend in the hearing of a teacher that this meant we would be getting a holiday. I was reprimanded for using the word "holiday;" school was closed because it was a day of mourning, we were told.

My happy schooling in Delhi came to an end rather abruptly when our family moved to Monghyr, a small town in Bihar on the Ganges, which had been flattened by a major earthquake in 1934. MK Gandhi famously described the earthquake as retribution for India's failure to eradicate untouchability. My father had contracts to rebuild Monghyr following the state of rubble to which it had been reduced. As an eleven-year old child, I found this to be a big adventure. We were told that cobras lurked under the rubble. To make up for being uprooted from our school and friends and moved to what appeared to be a remote part of the country, my brother and I were allowed to have pets. We got a pet monkey named Mankooo, a pony called Tony, and a dog named King.

Our house, with its large, sprawling garden of mango and lychee trees, was on the banks of the river Ganges. Being able to climb the trees, and pick fresh fruit, was great compensation for being relocated from Delhi and being apart from our old friends. An added treat came from having a boat and boatman to row us around to catch fish. When the river flooded over the monsoons, it would come right up to our verandah. The town nearest to Monghyr was Jamalpur, a British cantonment town where we could buy chocolates and other imported goodies. Canned peaches were a hot favorite and I adore them to this day.

As there were no schools, markets, medical facilities or other urban amenities, a tutor—Mr. Reddy—from South India, homeschooled us. He moved to Monghyr, took up residence in our compound and gave us a full-time education, based on the school curriculum. Mr. Reddy was a very good teacher, extremely demanding in terms of homework and punctuality. He made sure we listened and understood everything.

Patwant managed to skip classes often by feigning illness, which gave him the special advantage of gaining my parents' attention and extra treats. As a result, I received most of the benefit of Mr. Reddy's instruction and learned in two years what would have taken me four years in a regular school. This allowed me to sit for my matriculation examination at the age of thirteen, which was much younger than most other students. My subjects were the liberal arts and music, as well as math, which was compulsory but was my weakest subject. We had to travel to Patna for me to take the examination, a considerable distance, as there was no center in Monghyr. My matriculation coincided with the completion of Papaji's projects in Monghyr in 1936.

I passed the examination. Patwant preferred to take another year or two to settle down to studies. He tended to be as casual about them as I was determined. I therefore completed my school's final examination before I turned thirteen. Even as a young girl, I realized that education could be a pathway to the future that could ensure a career and economic independence.

two

AWAKENING TO A BIGGER WORLD

The family moved back to Delhi in 1936, when the burning issue of the day was India's independence. The freedom struggle dominated our lives and conversations. As our understanding of politics grew, we started identifying with the nationalist movement and considered our heroic national leaders our role models.

I especially admired Mahatma Gandhi and Jawaharlal Nehru. We spoke of them as if they were members of our family. Although they had sacrificed their personal lives and spent endless years in prison, this did not deflect them from their cause. I felt that Gandhi's philosophy of non-violent passive resistance—satyagraha—was the greatest political strategy ever devised. His hunger strikes became a powerful tool with which he finally achieved the goal of Indian independence, forcing the mighty British Empire to surrender what was often referred to as the jewel in its crown.

During those heady days, I began to move beyond the privileged environment in which I was raised and learn more about my country. I began traveling in third class compartments on Indian railways. I also began wearing *khadi*, home-spun cotton cloth, which Gandhi had advocated as a way of boycotting the fabrics manufactured by the factories of Lancashire. The British imported our cotton and exported the textiles manufactured in their mills back to India, generating great profit and dealing a severe blow to our country's own cloth manufacturing industry.

The profits from this trade enriched the British treasury, even as our own population could ill afford to buy these foreign fabrics.

In addition to male nationalist leaders, many eminent women filled me and my friends with patriotic fervor. I was deeply inspired by the extraordinary contributions of Sarojini Naidu, Kamladevi Chattopadhyay, Rajkumari Amrit Kaur, Aruna Asaf Ali, and Durgabai Deshmukh, all of whom were playing an active role in the freedom struggle. They were our role models.

The Congress party seemed committed to women's freedom. As early as 1939, Nehru had appointed a sub-committee on women's role in the planned economy for the national planning board. Its report stated unequivocally that women should be considered individuals who had the same political, civic, and legal rights as men; should enjoy social equality and economic independence and should share equally in the fruits of national development.

And yet I was not convinced that the Congress party would go far enough in eradicating class, caste, and gender inequality. Although Gandhi involved the masses in the struggle for independence and lived in neighborhoods demarcated for sweepers, invariably from the lower castes, Congress was dominated by elites and did not put the interests of peasants, workers, and women at the forefront of its agenda. To my mind the Communist Party of India was more committed to building an egalitarian society. I was inspired by several Communist leaders, including PC Joshi and Romesh Chandra. Although I never formally joined the Communist Party of India, I became what was then known as a "sympathizer." Soon I was attending the party's cell meetings at Jantar Mantar and at the Communist Party office in Jama Masjid, old Delhi, often bringing home banned party publications. Our house was once raided by the police looking for Communist literature. Fortunately, I had advance warning from my friends and co-workers and removed the offending material from the house.

Once World War II started, with Britain fighting on the side of the Allies, Indian soldiers were sent to several theatres of war and many of them sacrificed their lives to help their colonial masters. We regarded this war as an imperialist enterprise and believed that Indians were being exploited and victimized by being made to participate in it. However, when the USSR joined the Allies against the Axis powers, the Indian Communist Party declared that it was a "people's war" and claimed that it was our war as well.

I found this difficult to accept. After a year of being a Communist party sympathizer and a believer in socialist ideals, I just couldn't see how the war had suddenly become a "people's war." As Indians, we were still colonized by the British and had no say in the conduct of the war but were asked to extend blind allegiance and support to the Allies while sacrificing our own lives. I was also disappointed by how few women there were in leading roles in the Communist Party. A general disenchantment set in, leading me to sever connections with it.

Meanwhile I began attending the Indian National Army (INA) trials at Delhi's Red Fort, which involved the court martial of three courageous officers. They had fought alongside Subhas Chandra Bose on the eastern front because they believed that aligning with the Axis powers—Germany, Italy and Japan—was the more prudent course for India if it was to gain independence. The INA ranks comprised Indians living in Malaysia, Burma, and Singapore as well as soldiers captured by the Japanese. It had a female regiment of over 1,000 women, the Rani of Jhansi regiment, named after the legendary Indian queen who had fought the British in 1857. This was perhaps the first and only women's regiment in Indian history. It was headed by a medical doctor, Captain Lakshmi Sehgal. I was full of admiration, indeed in awe of her.

When the three legendary army officers—General Shah Nawaz Khan, Colonel Prem Sahgal, and Colonel Gurbaksh Singh Dhillon—stood trial, they were defended by the best legal minds in India, including Bhulabhai Desai and Jawaharlal Nehru. The latter donned his legal robes to argue on their behalf. I had no doubt that the officers were as committed as Congress members were to India's independence. Although I came to realize that the INA failed to appreciate the horrors of Germany's role in the Second World War, at the time, the fact that leaders were being tried as traitors really upset me.

Indian Independence finally arrived at midnight on August 15, 1947. I vividly recall listening over the radio to Nehru's memorable speech, "At the stroke of the midnight hour, when the world sleeps, India will awake to life and freedom. A moment comes, which comes but rarely in history, when we step out from the old to the new, when an age ends, and when the soul of a nation, long suppressed, finds utterance. It is fitting that at this solemn moment we take the pledge of dedication to the service of India and her people and to the still larger cause of humanity." The emotions that the speech evoked in us at that time are difficult to fully express. Every year thereafter, on January 26th we would hoist the Indian flag in college and pledge to continue the struggle for independence. India's freedom and our personal freedom were deeply intertwined.

Independence, however, came at the cost of a severely truncated India. On July 18, 1947, the British Parliament passed the Indian Independence Act, finalizing arrangements for a partition of the sub-continent, comprising 175,000 square miles of territory, into two separate nations, India and Pakistan. The arrangement was known as the Mountbatten Plan, named after the then Viceroy Lord Mountbatten. The border between India and Pakistan was determined by the Boundary Commission, that the British government created. The predominantly Hindu states remained with India. Pakistan comprised two Muslim-majority non-contiguous areas—western Punjab and the North West Frontier Province; and eastern Bengal. The two parts of Pakistan were separated by the Indian land mass. (In 1971, East Pakistan became Bangladesh, after a liberation struggle and war.)

Partition created huge challenges for 88 million people. It provoked the most massive exchange of populations between two countries ever to take place in world history. It is estimated that 14.5 million people crossed borders. The migrations were accompanied by untold violence and slaughter on both sides of the border, with estimates of the dead ranging from one half to one million. An additional 12 million were rendered homeless. India's capital city became home at the time to about a million refugees. Incredible displays of pain and anguish followed the expression of exhilaration and joy. I wished that Indian leaders had not agreed in such haste to the partition of India based on religion. It just seemed too big a price to pay for independence, both at the time and for future generations. Given the principles of nonviolence and passive resistance that had marked the freedom movement, if India's leaders had demonstrated patience, perhaps all the violence, pain and everlasting communal hostility in both countries might not have blotted the pages of our history. It was a terrible time in our history; the suffering on both sides of the border was indescribable.

The legacies of partition had a dramatic impact on our family. Our relatives were among the many Sikhs and Hindus who were forced to migrate from those parts of Punjab that became Pakistan. Once the killing and violence began and stories circulated about the dangers of remaining in what was now Pakistan, my father's parents, two of his brothers, their wives, his four sisters, their husbands, and all their children migrated to Delhi. They boarded the earliest available trains and headed to India laden with small bags carrying some valuables, a few clothes and what little cash they had in their houses. In Delhi, our home on Hanuman Road became a large refugee camp in which we provided food, shelter and safety to our relatives and others in need.

After coming to terms with the shock of parting from Rawalpindi—and their homes, friends, belongings and their lingering memories—my father's extended family gradually woke up to the permanence of their move. Because they had different ideas about where they would like to live, they gradually found their roots in cities like Ranchi, Nagpur, Jaipur, and Patna, scattered over northern and western India. Their decisions were based on the desire to be near my parents, in cities that were relatively congenial and where people spoke a familiar local language.

Ironically, it was at this very juncture that I was contemplating leaving India and my beloved city, Delhi, for an uncertain future. To understand how I came to contemplate this move, I need to retrace my steps. In 1936, I entered Indraprastha College, a women's college, where I studied liberal arts and majored in history. Entering college constituted a major transition in my life. Although I was much younger than my classmates, my parents allowed me to travel by public bus to and from college, and even hang out at the coffee house with women friends and visit their homes after classes during daylight hours.

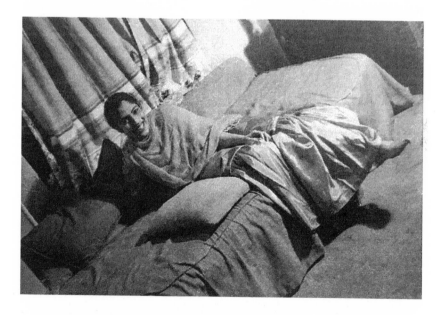

I made close friendships in college with some remarkable women. One was Sheila Uttam Singh, who later became the principal of the college. Another was the eminent scholar Rama Mehta. Before graduating from Indraprastha, I transferred to

Saint Stephen's College so I could enroll in an honors program and pursue an MA, neither of which Indraprastha College offered. Saint Stephen's was a very prestigious men's college, modeled on Oxford and Cambridge, and exuded a similar elitist snobbishness. Having long been a bastion of male exclusivity, it had just opened its portals to women. My parents, who were initially uneasy with the idea of my attending a predominantly male institution, eventually came around to the idea.

There were only a handful of women in Saint Stephen's. Classes were small, intense, and demanded concentrated attention. Girls sat in the front row, under the vigilant eyes of the professors, who saw to it that the boys did not heckle or harass us. In addition to the regular curriculum, we had to take two electives. I chose the rather unusual combination of auto mechanics and Sikh history. I also learned to drive, something that wasn't common for women at that time, but it came in handy when I later drove across the United States.

My social life was restricted to hanging out after classes in the India Coffee House in Connaught Place with women friends. Now and then a few male classmates would join us and we would go to the movies together but there was no serious dating. We may have had crushes but our relationships were completely platonic.

My studies at Saint Stephen's boosted my confidence. I took part in school debates, which were invariably centered on political issues. It was perhaps my debating skills that made me increasingly consider studying law after completing my liberal arts studies. I decided that an MA in History would be a precursor to legal studies. That way, teaching could be a fallback option in case the legal profession didn't work out.

My conviction grew that if I wanted to be independent, I would need to break the accepted pattern of getting married after graduating. I simply had to have a career. My great passions at this point were to fight gender discrimination, have a profession, and be financially independent. Like my friends, I believed that

all sorts of possibilities would open up for women after India achieved independence.

However, there were few options for young women at that time. The accepted professions were teaching, medicine, and social work. Medicine, in particular gynecology and obstetrics, was acceptable because women preferred female doctors. The legal profession was not considered an option. Although there were no formal barriers to women gaining admission to law schools or practicing law, social norms discouraged women from becoming lawyers. But I wanted to be in the vanguard of change.

Law school was not very academically challenging but I loved moot court, studied hard, and expanded my horizons. I was something of a curiosity—there was only one other female student in the school, and about one thousand men.

My life changed after I completed my law examination. The Vice Chancellor of Delhi University, an Englishman by the name of Maurice Gwyer, offered me an appointment in the law faculty at Delhi University, on condition that I score a first division in the law examination. The results of the examination were not yet out. Sir Gwyer was to retire before the next term. His offer created a real predicament. Innumerable questions raced through my head. If I did well and got the job, would I be able to maintain discipline in class and teach students who were just a year or two junior to me? Would I, a young woman in a predominantly men's school, be able to control classes of 50 to 60 students? In the worst-case scenario, if my results weren't satisfactory, would I be disgraced by not getting the appointment? What sort of a career would I have then?

After pondering hard, I thought of an honorable exit strategy, which was to study abroad, preferably in the U.S., for a Master's in Law (LLM). I decided against going to Britain as I feared that it would be too racist. I believed America was a freer country and one where I would have more opportunities. But where was I to start? And how would I persuade my parents to let me go? After all, I was young, led a protected life, and had never lived away from home—not even in a girls' boarding school.

An unexpected opportunity came my way during my summer vacation in Mussoorie, a resort hill station built by the British in the Himalayas. I made friends with two American women who were staying in the same hotel as my family. Christine Weston was an Anglo-French novelist who had spent her early childhood in India and Anne Johnson was a Yale Law School graduate who worked in Washington D.C. As soon as Anne told me about the most prestigious law schools, I drafted letters of enquiry to Yale, Harvard, and Columbia.

Around this time, the law school examination results were announced. Not only did I top the list but I was awarded a gold medal for the most distinguished student in the history of the Delhi Law School. My appointment in the Law Faculty was confirmed. Since I had not yet heard from the American law schools, I began preparing my lectures.

Having a female professor was quite a novelty for the students. Many day-students behaved like male chauvinists by ignoring me or acting rude. I had better luck with evening students who had office jobs and wanted to improve their career prospects by getting a law degree. They were generally older and more motivated than the day students. After all, they had to pay the tuition fees from their own pocket, whereas most day students were younger, financially supported by their parents, and lacked motivation.

There was one other woman on the faculty, Lotika Mitra, who became Lotika Sarkar after her marriage. The sharpness of her mind struck me at the time, and she became a very close friend. I stayed with her parents, who were stationed in London, on my first trip abroad. Lotika later emerged as one of the leading lights of feminist activism in India and was part of the team that authored the landmark Status of Women Committee Report in 1974. A great legal activist and feminist, she continued to teach at the Law Faculty for decades thereafter, inspiring generations of students. But Lotika was the exception that proved the rule; it was highly unusual for a woman to teach at the law school.

I quickly settled down in my teaching routine. I forgot all about the escape route that I had planned to the United States. Eight months into my teaching career, I received a reply to my Harvard application from the Dean of the Law School. He wrote: "We have read your letter with great interest. You'll be shocked, and justifiably so, to know we don't admit women." I was indeed shocked to find such blatant discrimination against women in the U.S. However, several months later, I got a response from Yale which restored my faith in American academia. Yale Law School was not only willing to admit me but also informed me that I was eligible for a prestigious Sterling Fellowship in Law.

Once again, I faced a dilemma. I was enjoying my teaching job and worried about resigning after such a short period. My life had settled into a comfortable groove. Faculty colleagues were very friendly and sociable and encouraged me to discuss any problems I might encounter. After initial problems with students who tried to trip me up in silly ways or to flout my authority by reading newspapers in class, my professional life had settled into a steady rhythm. Moreover, I was sure that my parents would never agree to my going to the U.S. alone. After obtaining one law degree, I suspected they would claim that I had studied enough. They undoubtedly thought that it was time for me, now twenty-four, to marry and start a family. They were already hunting for a suitable match and had identified a pilot in the Indian Air Force. However, I told them firmly that he was just not my type. The gentleman in question went on to become a national hero after breaking a number of flying records. Unfortunately, he was later killed in a plane crash.

After tormenting myself for weeks, I decided to pursue the Yale alternative. I had to work on three fronts: convince my parents to allow me to go; persuade the Delhi Law School to grant me a leave of absence; and ensure that Yale granted me the Sterling Fellowship. With persistence and good fortune I succeeded on all three fronts—an indication that when I set my mind on something, I could not be deterred. My parents agreed, not only to my going, but to paying for my travel, board, lodging and other expenses. My tuition was covered by the Sterling Fellowship. The Delhi Law School agreed to grant me a one-year leave. I was admitted to Yale to begin my studies in the fall of 1948, just before my 25th birthday. As Winston Churchill stated—about a more dangerous situation: this was not the end nor even the beginning of the end; but it could be considered the end of the beginning.

three

MAKING A HOME IN AMERICA

In September 1948 I left my home and parents in Delhi to take the P&O ocean liner from Bombay to Southampton. I felt completely lost and kept wondering whether I had made the right decision. My contemporaries seemed content in Delhi, settling for the comforts of domesticity, and this led me to ask myself why I needed to go so far from home. Although Papaji had accepted my decision, parting with Mamaji was fraught. She was clearly torn between wanting me to achieve my full potential and her own inclination that favored marriage as the better option for her daughter. I have been left ever since with a feeling that I had let down my mother, rich and rewarding as my life has been.

Bombay was the first halt on what was my first journey outside the country. I was met there by my brother, Patwant, who had moved to Bombay to join my father in the construction business. His interest in buildings was to lead him to writing and publishing on architecture, laying the foundation for his lifelong commitment to civic design and conservation. Patwant invited me to stay overnight as his guest at the iconic Taj Hotel and it was an enormous treat. The Taj was (and still is) one of the finest hotels in India at the time and was even designated as one of the world's best. Of course, it was very expensive but it certainly proved to be a memorable break. From my hotel window I could see the Gateway of India and cars heading to the causeway. Bombay was a bustling metropolis with a vast public transport system—a total contrast to Delhi, which was considered at that time a village by comparison.

The ship was scheduled to leave the next day. As luck would have it, we received news of a cholera outbreak in Cairo, where the ship was to dock for about twelve hours. This meant that the departure from Bombay had to be delayed and it was by no means clear how long it would be before we sailed. It turned out to be five days.

Patwant and me picnicking with friends

Patwant had been invited to visit some friends, Gurcharan and Ranjit Singh, to their elegant home in Pune, and they added me to the guest list. Patwant and I readily agreed. We were welcomed warmly and were looked after in great style. The days in Pune went by far too quickly and before long we were driving back to Bombay, where the ship was finally ready to sail. Patwant must have heaved a sigh of relief to know that he didn't have to pay for another night at the Taj hotel, although I believe he was a bit sad to see me leave the nest.

The boat was very elegant, with elaborate meals, a live band and dancing. Everyone dressed in formal clothes for drinks and then dinner. There were all kinds of sports on the decks—ping pong, billiards and croquet—as well as a good library. Most importantly, there were a number of other young passengers, many of whom were heading to England to study. We became friends and went sight-seeing when the ship docked at Port Said, our first stop. We took buses from there to Cairo. What an exciting city it was. While most men wore embroidered *abayas* (cloaks), I spotted many women in western clothes. The bazaars were bustling with goods and vendors, shops were stacked high with silver, brass and copper bowls, pots and pans, and the most exquisitely carved samovars that appeared straight out of the Arabian Nights. We visited the Cairo Museum, which proved to be an eye opener, with history literally unfolding before you. The mummies stared point blank at us and among them was Queen Nefertiti in all her beauty. The pyramids came next and I remember thinking that the Sphinx was as inscrutable as I had imagined. Riding on camels took us to a higher elevation, from where we didn't have to crane our necks to see these wondrous sights. Tea at the Mena House Hotel provided a refreshing break, after which we had to rush back to the boat. Cairo was a dream come true.

Our journey resumed and the ship moved slowly through the Suez Canal to the Mediterranean. Although it stopped briefly at Gibraltar, we weren't allowed to disembark. Two weeks went by rather quickly and before I knew it we had arrived in Southampton, our final destination. I gathered my bags and rushed to catch the train to London, where I was staying with Lotika's parents.

I had long heard about the famous landmarks of London and I could now take in all the familiar sights captured in postcards, magazines and biscuit boxes: the red double-decker buses, the guards outside Buckingham Palace in their black fur hats, the

Tower of London, the River Thames, Westminster Abbey, and of course the Houses of Parliament and Big Ben. Despite the post-war shortages, Londoners seemed to be doing just fine; here's where the legendary stiff upper lip of the British must have helped.

The wonderful week in London passed by in a rush as I tried to see and absorb everything. Soon it was time to leave for New Haven. That flight from Heathrow, London, to New York's Idlewild airport (later renamed Kennedy airport), was to be my first journey by air and it was therefore momentous in its own way. Once we touched down, I planned to take a taxi to Grand Central Station and board the train to New Haven.

What filled me with trepidation was that I didn't know a soul in the U.S. Christine had given me an introduction to her mother, who lived in Pleasantville, New Jersey, and Anne had sent me her address in Washington D.C., where she was to arrive a few months later. Outside the airport I hailed a taxi to take me to the train station. "Which one?" the cab driver asked. I didn't have a clue, not even knowing there was more than one. "For the train to New Haven," I pronounced gamely. He drove me to Grand Central Station, which was a universe in itself. I saw shops and kiosks selling all kinds of food items, books, magazines, and newspapers. People milled around but there was no sign of trains. I looked in vain for porters to carry my bags as they did back home, but eventually had to lug them myself to the information counter, where I was directed to another counter where I could buy my ticket for New Haven. In those days the exchange rate was twelve rupees to a dollar. I had with me a small sum of dollars for initial expenses and tried to make them go a long way through careful management, although nobody at home ever thought I was good with handling money.

Two hours later I found myself in New Haven, in the company of women who were responsible for hospitality. Mrs. Sturges, the wife of the Dean of the Law School and several other faculty wives met me at the station. They dropped me at the graduate dorm for women, since the Law School residences were for men only. The graduate dorm was off campus and there was no place to eat. We had to walk to the cafeteria on campus, which was fifteen minutes by foot, or settle for little restaurants or diners, which were some distance from the dorm. To my astonishment, women were not allowed to enter the law school dining hall from the front entrance: we had to use the back door. For me, this was an early introduction to institutionalized gender discrimination. I soon discovered that everything was weighted in favor of men, in both academics and in sports.

Several aspects of social life on campus intrigued or disquieted me. I felt totally isolated during inter-university football matches between ivy league teams. Although I got invited to football games by a few students, it was difficult to get sufficiently interested to spend an entire day at the games. I also missed the cricket and tennis matches in Delhi, which I had thoroughly enjoyed.

In the graduate LLM classes there were only two other foreign women—one from Cuba and the other from Mexico. Although the LLB program had more women, they constituted a small minority. The other thing that struck me immediately was that while Indian students were very politicized from an early age by the Independence movement, Yale students appeared apathetic about politics and political engagement. Most of them were older and quite a few were World War II veterans. They had joined the Law School under the Serviceman's Readjustment Act of 1944, popularly known as the G.I. Bill. Veterans were eligible for, among other things, state support for college tuition and living expenses.

However, the faculty and their wives were warm and welcoming and classes went smoothly except for the initial difficulty with comprehending American accents and the maddening acronyms for various regulatory federal agencies and other institutions. What was most gratifying, was the education I received. The Yale Law School at that time was in the process of developing its own distinctive approach, the McDougal-Lasswell approach to

law. Simply put, it was based on the thesis that law was a product of society and socially relevant, and therefore demanded an integrated, holistic, multidisciplinary approach. For example, the mock courts for our criminal law classes brought in people who had been incarcerated along with psychologists, sociologists, anthropologists and public officials, all of whom offered their perspectives on crime. Communication was for the first time introduced as a subject in the law courses. It was taught by Harold Lasswell, a pioneer scholar in political science and communication theory. Other illustrious professors whose courses I took included Felix Cohen, who fundamentally shaped Native American law and offered a course on jurisprudence, and Thomas Emerson, a legal theorist and a major architect of civil rights law, who taught administrative and constitutional law. More traditional law schools like Harvard quipped that Yale taught everything but law.

I enjoyed the informality of the classroom and especially the seminar system, which did not exist at Delhi University, where we had to memorize and cram for exams. Our history instruction included no room for interpretation or analysis. At Yale, we had lively discussions, which encouraged us to think for ourselves and develop analytical skills. A thorough familiarity with case law was essential because that formed the precedents for future court decisions.

My first exposure to New York society came when a Yale Law School friend, Mary Jones, invited me to her mother's Fifth Avenue apartment to join her family and friends for Thanksgiving. We sat down to a lavish traditional dinner which I found exotic. It consisted of turkey with stuffing, several vegetables and varieties of bread, with pumpkin, mince and apple pies as dessert

Mary took me to all the tourist sights of New York. We strolled on Fifth Avenue and Madison Avenue, and visited Greenwich Village and Chinatown. I could not get over the super-abundance of everything—the vast array of consumer goods, restaurants, skyscrapers and the enormous public transport network. How smoothly everything worked. Though Christmas was a month away, the lights and decorations were already adorning storefronts and carols were being sung everywhere. Little did I know that New York would become my future home.

I have often heard visitors say New York is a great place to visit but they couldn't live there. True, it is intimidating. But those who do live there say they couldn't live anywhere else. By comparison, every other city is a small town, lacking New York's color, heterogeneity and electric charge. Though it appears impersonal, it has the spirit of neighborhood in most residential areas. Lacking the beauty of Paris or the splendors of Rome or the graciousness of London, New York makes up for it by its energy, informality, and feeling of home to newcomers.

Back in New Haven, it was time to work on term papers, which had to be submitted before the end of the fall semester. During the Christmas holidays, I divided my time between friends' homes and catching up on my reading and academic work at Yale.

That first summer, a great vacation and adventure awaited me after I read a notice on the student bulletin board posted by Ruth Carter, a secretary in the Institute of Pacific Relations (IPR) in New York. The IPR was an NGO devoted to research and policy in the Pacific region. Ruth's boss, Bill Holland, wanted her to deliver his car to San Francisco, where he had moved. Ruth wanted company, as well as help with the expenses and driving. She had been contacted by two students from Princeton University, Mac and John, but she also wanted a woman companion. When I learned of the possibility, I immediately took a course to get an American driver's license so that I could share driving with the other three. The two boys from Princeton knew each other but I was a stranger to all three. After I had my driver's license, and was accepted into the group, we set off from New York.

It was wonderful to be free and mobile and drive from coast to coast seeing this vast country. It took us five days to get from New York to San Francisco. We drove during the day, stopping for meals and to visit places of interest. We slept in motels. We had a few adventures on the way. As we passed the vast stretch of salt flats in Bonneville, Utah, we were inspired by stories of cars that drove through them and broke all speed records. We got off the highway to drive on the flats, but no sooner had we done so then our car got stuck in the sand and salt. The more we tried to drive out, the deeper it sank. Panic set in as we were in the middle of nowhere. There were no cars in sight to flag down and of course this was long before the era of cell phones. We waited patiently on the side of the road for what appeared to be forever. About an hour later, a car approached. Seeing our predicament, the driver agreed to ask at the next gas station for a truck to be dispatched to tow the car out. Eventually we were free to continue on our way.

We had another adventure in Reno, Nevada, where we tried our luck at gambling. The casinos were an eye-opener—dazzling spaces with bright lights, filled with intense men and women who were grimly intent on making a fast buck. I chose the slot machines and roulette, without any luck. My friends met with the same fate. We were soon too broke to go to a hotel, so we had dinner and kept driving. Our next stop was Lake Tahoe, a beautiful lake surrounded by beaches. We slept on its bank in our sleeping bags, resuming our journey the next morning.

In San Francisco, the four of us parted company after an elegant cocktail party hosted by Mac's friends. Ruth took up work with IPR in San Francisco, while John and Mac visited friends. I stayed at the International House in Berkeley. I met a few Indian students there. Ishwar, who was studying philosophy in Berkeley, took me around the beautiful city, with its Golden Gate Bridge, museums, galleries, the harbor and Chinatown. I loved San Francisco and wished I could have spent more time exploring the city.

Los Angeles was totally different, with its many high rises and fast pace. The star attraction for me was Hollywood. On the train from San Francisco to Los Angeles, I met a member of the Disney family, who invited me to visit the Disney Studios, which I was so eager to see. Not only was I given a tour of the studio, but I was invited to eat at the executive dining room.

Indians were a rarity in the U.S. in those days. I attracted a lot of attention because I wore a sari. Initially I felt very self-conscious and wished to merge with the crowd, but after awhile I got used to it. Often people stopped me on the street to ask where I came from and what my costume was called.

After a few days in LA, I boarded a Greyhound bus to visit the Grand Canyon. I sat next to a lovely young woman who told me that she was also Indian. I asked her where in India she was from. She replied that she was an American Indian from a reservation not far from the Grand Canyon. She invited me to her home and presented me with a beautiful silver bracelet set with turquoise stones. Her parents did not speak English but were very hospitable and warm. Later, back on the bus, I was awed by scenery that overshadowed the man-made canyons, the skyscrapers of New York. Tourists were heading by ponies or on foot down to camp at the valley below. Not having time to stop there, I had to content myself with watching the varying colors of the rock formations in the morning light and at sunset. I saw artists and art students trying to capture the magnificence of the Canyon on canvas. One artist invited me to stay overnight in her beautiful adobe house, which I did. From the Grand Canyon I took the Greyhound bus back to New York and New Haven by the southern route.

While this trip was an experience of a lifetime, another unexpected opportunity that came my way during the summer vacation, proved to be the turning point in my life. The UN intern division asked the Law School to recommend students to participate in its six-week internship program. The program was designed to attract graduate students or young professionals to work in the different departments of the UN after acquainting themselves with its ideals and objectives. The goal was to have them return to their respective countries and convey knowledge about the UN and its values.

I chose to intern in the Human Rights Division. In those early days, the UN was located in Lake Success on Long Island, in temporary headquarters provided by Sperry's Gyroscope Company. It was a sprawling single-story structure near Great Neck, about an hour's drive from New York. Only in 1952 did the UN find a permanent location at the present site overlooking the East River in New York.

Initially the interns were housed at Adelphi College, near the UN. There were 20 of us representing different regions and continents. I looked up notices on the bulletin board in the UN Secretariat for longer-term housing. There were several places that advertised vacancies but when I called, sometimes just hours after the notices had been posted, I was told that the rooms were no longer available. I suspected that the landlords were racist. I finally found a place to rent in a house owned by a woman called Celia Weinberg. It was a pleasant room on the second floor. I visited the house with my friend Romen. Celia assumed that I did not speak English because I was wearing a sari. She said to him, "Please explain the terms to her. The rent has to be paid each week. There's a deposit. And she can use the kitchen for light cooking." Celia Weinberg turned out to be warm and friendly, a real "Jewish mother." Her son, Wiff (Irving), and daughter-in-law, Martha, also became dear friends as did their children and grand-children, who visited me in India.

At the end of the internship, I returned to Yale, completed my LLM, and said good bye to my friends and professors. I enrolled in a six-week course at the International Academy of Law at The Hague and found myself in a setting very different from New York. I would bicycle to the Academy every day from the place where I was staying.

After completing the program and getting my certificate from the Hague, I returned to New York, and was soon homeward bound for New Delhi. I was at a crossroads in my life and had to make some serious decisions about my future. I did well at Yale Law School and graduated with honors in the LLM program. Yale

At a meeting of UN Interns with Eleanor Roosevelt

offered me a scholarship to write my doctoral thesis on the Legal Status of Aliens in the British Commonwealth of Nations. My three options were: returning to teaching at the Delhi Law School, from where I was still on leave; returning to Yale Law School to do a Ph.D. in international law; and applying for a position in the UN Division of Human Rights.

Career-wise, my inclination was to try for a job in the UN Secretariat. My parents, of course, wanted me in Delhi with them, to resume teaching law and hopefully get married to a Sikh gentleman.

Initially, I resumed teaching at the Delhi Law School. But in a short time, I received a job offer from the UN for a professional position in the Human Rights Division. This meant that I now had to negotiate with my parents and the Delhi Law School to get them on board. They both reluctantly agreed to my accepting the position after I assured them that it would be temporary.

By the time I returned to New York, the UN was preparing to move to its permanent location in New York City. My office, the Human Rights Division, was the first to be moved. The entire ambiance and working environment were totally different from the temporary headquarters. I had a lovely office on the 31st floor. I was proud to have an office with three windows facing the East River, which I shared with Clara Belshaw, another staff member.

With Clara Belshaw, my UN office mate

I immersed myself in my new responsibilities, drafting reports on the state of human rights in different countries. It was demanding, challenging but exhilarating work and the start of my lifelong career at the UN.

UN Cooperative Service Station Opens at Headquarters

four

CREATING NEW HOMES IN THE WORLD

It was at the start of my internship at the UN that I met my future husband, Romen Basu, a Bengali from Calcutta, who was working as a professional at the UN. I had only a few male friends and Romen struck me as particularly warm, gregarious and friendly. He was also a persistent suitor. While I was doing an internship at the Hague, Romen, who was posted in Bangkok at the time, would call the Academy every morning while I was in class and someone would announce, "Mr. Basu is on the phone for you." I thought he was much too daring.

On another occasion, the UN had arranged for a group of interns to visit Ottawa, Montreal, Toronto, and Quebec City in Canada. The trip gave us a great opportunity to interact with other interns and see a different part of North America. Romen scrutinized the Canadian newspapers for a mention of our tour. When he spotted a picture of us in a Toronto paper, he rented a car, drove up to Canada, called the newsroom and asked where we were staying. The next morning, when I came down for breakfast, there he was. As they say, the rest is history.

Romen and I had very different personalities. He tended to be emotional, passionate and demonstrative. The children would later recall how he would greet me on returning home from work with the words, "Hello Mrs., love and kisses." I, in contrast, was more low-key and reserved.

Romen began thinking about marriage early in our relationship. He often repeated his proposal to me, each time asking, "Rasil, will you marry me?" Every time he popped the question he would add, "Would this try make the cut?" I would then playfully retort, "Surely you can do better. Put some more passion into your words." Over time, I changed my response to: "I'm considering it." Finally, I agreed. I was charmed by Romen's vivaciousness and love of life. We got married on October 28, 1951.

Before we got married, Romen went to Delhi to meet my parents, making sure to stay in a well-appointed hotel close to their residence. They liked this young man from New York but had no idea that he was to be their future son-in-law, since neither he nor I had told them that we planned to get married. When I finally summoned the courage to write and tell them, they were, as I feared, far from happy. Mamaji, particularly, had always wanted me to marry within the Sikh community and settle down in Delhi. They did not approve of my marrying a Hindu from Calcutta and

Papaji and Romen

living in New York. While Papaji and Maaji continued to correspond with me, Mamaji was so upset that she didn't write to me for a year after my marriage. All this left me torn, aware that my decision to marry Romen had hurt my mother so grievously. For me, it was a period filled with apprehension and guilt. But I felt assured of Romen's devotion to me through it all. Things were much less fraught when it came to Romen's family. His mother had passed away years earlier, and his father and uncle were not particularly opposed to the union.

Our marriage ceremony in New York was a simple affair. Romen and I went to the home of a local judge, the father-in-law of a friend and colleague, Karl Graf, to sign the papers to register our marriage. Romen gave me an unadorned platinum ring to seal the moment. I have worn it all my life and even today it sits on the index finger of my left hand. My landlady and dear friend, Celia, was a witness at my marriage. The high point of my wedding day was a dinner at a fashionable restaurant on Park Avenue. There were just three of us—Romen, Celia, and me, and we made a lovely evening of it.

Cutting our wedding cake

In keeping with our love of travel, we planned an exciting honeymoon to Bermuda, which in those days was a British outpost. After visiting the British Colonial Office in New York for travel authorization, we made a booking at a very nice hotel. Once we landed there, however, we were told that the booking had not come through and we could not be accommodated. After two or three other hotels in Bermuda turned us down, we realized that we were being subjected to racism, pure and simple. We were hurt and outraged. We eventually rented a room at a lovely little place by the beach, hired bicycles and enjoyed ourselves. But we also made it a point to visit the Colonial Office and file a formal complaint over the treatment meted out to us. We also informed the UN about it when we returned home. The UN authorities informed the British Colonial Office that they took the matter very seriously.

With Romen, after marriage

There were other opportunities to travel in our newlywed days. Romen was in the United Nations Department of Technical Cooperation to Developing Countries. In the course of his work, he came across a Chinese shipping magnate, who wanted to set up a floating university that had attracted many interesting academics. One of those was Norman Young, a well-known Left-leaning writer. Through him, we got to travel on the ship to several regions around the world. I especially remember visiting Kenya, where we took a safari. The ship finally berthed outside Hong Kong harbor and the university took shape. Sadly, Norman died shortly after our trip and the people who inherited the ship were not excited by the prospect of running a university on it.

Another trip, soon after marriage, was to Calcutta, to meet Romen's family. His family was very different from mine. It was a large extended Bengali household of about 50 members who all lived together in a large home. There were certain norms observed within the family that were non-negotiable, including that the men always got to eat first and the women would serve them. As the new daughter-in-law, I was required to get up early in the morning, cover my head with my *pallu* (the end of the sari), and touch the feet of the elders. The family also expected me to cook a good mutton dish.

Although I was not used to doing any of these things, I tried initially to comply. Romen was really not much support in such matters. He would shrug his shoulders and say, "It is what it is. Welcome to the Bengali household." I would struggle with the mutton and finally asked the cook to help chop up the meat and cook it. Luckily our first visit coincided with the Durga Puja holiday, and as luck would have it, the family driver went on leave just at that point. This meant that the family now had to turn to me to drive them around. I made clear that I could not drive with my sari covering my head.

In New York, Romen and I settled down to the life of a working couple. Since I did not know how to cook, we survived initially

Romen's extended family

on sandwiches and pizzas bought from neighborhood outlets. Romen, it turned out, was a good cook and I was more than willing to concede this role to him. Fortunately, he accepted my failings on the domestic front as a marker of the modern woman.

When I became pregnant a year later, it came as a bit of a shock. I would have liked to have waited a bit before having our first child, but we had taken no precautions, reflecting perhaps the mix of naivete and sophistication that marked our ways. Romen and I were attending the Metropolitan Opera in a standing-room-only space when my water broke, and we had to be rushed to the hospital, much to the surprise of the other attendees.

Our first-born arrived 24 hours later. We named her Amrita, after the famous modern Indian artist, Amrita Sher-Gil, whose work and independent lifestyle I admired greatly. Amrita Sher-Gil's father was Sikh and perhaps that was another link. By a strange quirk of fate, our home in Delhi was on a street named Ratendon Road which was later renamed Amrita Sher-Gil Marg.

Little Amrita helped re-establish my relationship with Mamaji. She was delighted by having a grandchild and began to write to me once again.

Although I got maternity leave from the UN, caring for a baby was an intimidating proposition. Despite my love for the little one, I knew I needed help. So, when Romen told me that the baby was my responsibility, I hired a nurse. It strained the household budget considerably, but it was such a relief to have Mrs. Jones around. She took over the baby and the household completely and helped tide me over that difficult initial period. I was able to continue hiring a nanny while working.

Since Romen worked in the Technical Cooperation program, he was required to travel to different countries. He had four long-term field assignments. The first was to Egypt (1954-1955), followed by stints in Libya (1957-1958), Delhi (1960-62), and Bangkok (1962-1965). When the Egypt posting came, the UN Secretariat pressured me to resign from my job, refusing to find a position for me in a UN agency in Egypt. It cited anti-nepotism rules although these should not have applied to me since I was already employed in the UN when we got married. Finally, after a lot of debate, they agreed to grant me leave without pay. The same situation occurred each time Romen took up long-term postings. Despite my permanent contract, I was always pressured to put my career and earnings on hold. This limited my salary and meant that I would never be promoted to the rank I would have otherwise achieved. My case was not unique: this was the experience of many UN women employees at that time. This fueled my determination to work for women's rights both within and beyond the UN system.

After Romen left for Cairo, I had a difficult time combining the responsibilities of motherhood and career in New York and to make the commute from home to work every day. Once my leave without pay was approved, therefore, I immediately left for Cairo with Amrita, who had become increasingly active.

Romen's first Cairo assignment was working under Dr. Walter Sharp, a UN Consultant posted there, who headed the School of Public Administration at Yale. A team of three under Dr. Sharp's supervision was assisting and advising the Egyptian government on projects launched between the revolution of 1952 and the presidency of Gamel Abdel Nasser, in 1956.

We stayed in a hotel when we first moved to Cairo and I sought to juggle the responsibilities of parenting with enjoying this wonderful city. I still vividly recall leaving Amrita in the care of one of the hotel attendants when Romen and I went out for dinner one evening. When we returned, the room was empty. Alarmed, we rushed down to the front desk to find out what had happened. After a frantic search we found the attendant with Amrita on the roof top. He had taken her there to stop her from crying.

Living in Cairo was a comfortable existence for us—almost luxurious by New York standards—with a well-equipped apartment with modern amenities. Romen was happy with his job and we quickly settled in our apartment in the lovely Zamlek neighborhood. A nanny joined the household. We also found a good cook, which gave me plenty of free time. Romen and I became members of the Gezira Sports Club where we would play tennis, badminton, table tennis and billiards with other young couples. Bridge was the other popular option. When Romen was at work, I would spend pleasant hours lunching with friends—both Egyptians and expatriate women, taking along Amrita. There was a children's playground in the neighborhood, where the nannies took their young charges. While the children played, the nannies caught up with the latest gossip.

Cairo reminded me somewhat of Bombay—a big, bustling city combining the splendors of the old and new worlds, the comforts of the West and the luxuries of the East. There were fine cafes, restaurants and patisseries. As in Bombay, traffic was dense. The pace of life, however, changed during the weekends and on holidays, and we would seize these leisure hours to go on cruises down the Nile for picnics, take motoring trips to the pyramids and have long lunches at the Mena House hotel overlooking them. That was where I had had tea during my first visit to Cairo as a student many years earlier.

One of the highlights of our stay in Cairo was the visit of Indian Prime Minister Jawaharlal Nehru. These were the early days of India's nation-building and we were still luxuriating in the afterglow of independence. We were so proud of the leaders who had fought for freedom and the very idea of meeting Nehru in person was exhilarating. We were among members of the Indian community in Cairo who were invited to a small reception with him at the Indian High Commission. Nehru was very good looking and personable. I was holding Amrita, who was a little over a year old in my arms and she was clutching a rose for him. He greeted us cordially, accepted the rose and placed it on his lapel. It was a memorable moment. Had it happened today, we may have managed a selfie.

The Cairo days went by quickly. While I loved going out with friends, I had had some reservations about leaving Amrita alone with the nanny for stretches of time, as she had been coming down with fevers and stomach ailments. There was a trained gynecologist and obstetrician I used to consult named Dr. Walters. I took Amrita to him for a medical opinion and what he told me was alarming. Her fevers and stomach upsets were probably caused by opium. Many local nannies, it seems, were sedating their little charges with small doses of opium so they wouldn't cry. Dr. Walters also examined me, and to my surprise he found that I was pregnant.

Both pieces of information helped me make up my mind: I did not want to leave Amrita in the charge of the nanny any longer and, although Dr. Walters assured me that I would be well cared for during pregnancy and childbirth in Cairo, I was determined to return with Amrita to Delhi to have the baby. By the time I left Cairo for my parents' home in Delhi, I was already over eight months pregnant. I was not supposed to fly, but the sari is a great

Papaji, Amrita, and me at our Amrita Sher-Gil Marg home

disguise for large bellies. I managed to circumvent the rule and land safely in Delhi.

It was good to be back home under the care of my family. We had our second daughter in a small nursing home which operated strictly under the natural childbirth regimen. We named her Rekha, a Bengali name that Romen chose. Rekha was a quiet and easy baby, except for the bouts of colic that she and Amrita experienced in the evenings. By the time she was born, I had become a more relaxed mother and was not as worried by the baby's crying.

While son-preference was very strong in the society of that time, I loved the idea of being the mother to two daughters, imagining what good friends they would be to each other as they grew up. Romen's father had wanted a grandson and had instructed Romen to send him a telegram if it was a boy. If it was another girl, he instructed, there was no need to waste money; a letter would do. Romen, however, insisted on our going to Calcutta by train when Rekha was just a week old, and his father proved to be an extremely affectionate grandfather to both our children. The extended family attended to our every need.

Amrita, Rekha, and me with friends

After Romen's Cairo assignment was over, our family returned to New York City. My housekeeping skills were still rudimentary and meeting the needs of two growing children was tough. I turned to magazines like Woman's Day and Family Circle for quick and easy recipes like chicken a la King made with canned creamed soup and jello with tinned fruit.

We got our gourmet fare on weekends, when Romen occupied the kitchen. He would pamper the girls by asking them what nationality food they wanted, then visit grocery stores in ethnic neighborhoods like Chinatown and turn out delicious meals from that country's culinary repertoire.

I resumed work at the UN, but not for long. Two years later, Romen was again given an overseas assignment, this time to Libya. Once again, I had to confront the dilemma of persuading the UN to grant me a leave without pay. Initially I stayed in New

With Amrita, Rekha, and Champa Chahil

York, coping as best as I could as a single mother of two, while awaiting a decision. A year's leave was finally granted, and I left with the girls to join Romen in Benghazi.

Libya, made up of the provinces of Cyrenaica, Tripolitania, and Fezzan, had declared itself a constitutional monarchy under King Idris in 1951, just six years before we moved there. The North African nation had been colonized by Italy, which dubbed it Albya and relinquished all claims to it in 1947.

To a student of history like me, there was much about Libya that was fascinating. Several important Greek and Persian ruins were found in the province of Cyrenaica and the city of Cyrene itself was founded by ancient Greeks in 630 BC. About a hundred years later, it was conquered by the Persians and remained under Persian and Egyptian rule for two centuries. The province of Fezzan, however, was under the virtual control of the Berber tribes of the hinterland, who accepted Islam but resented Arab rule.

In deference to these different histories and in accordance with the agreement signed between Italy and Britain at the time of the formation of the kingdom, Libya's capital rotated every year between Tripoli and Benghazi. During our posting in 1958 it was Benghazi's turn to be the capital city, which was a shame for us, because it was a dreary British cantonment town. By contrast, Tripoli was by all accounts a cosmopolitan Italian city with a lot of character and charm. Unfortunately, I never got a chance to visit it.

The UN considered Libya a hardship posting and I soon realized why. It was an extremely patriarchal society. In deference to the social and cultural mores, even non-Libyan women could not be visible in public, except perhaps in the meat and vegetable markets. There were no restaurants or movie theaters and the one British-style club was only open to men.

Romen had to conform to local norms. He put in long hours at work and was obliged to attend official and social events that were strictly for men in the evenings. The best I could do was to visit the market, demurely dressed, for a leg of lamb or a limited choice of fruits and vegetables

Romen tried hard to make life in Benghazi attractive by renting a nice villa before we arrived. The exciting feature of the house was that it shared a boundary wall with the city zoo. This took some getting used to as the lions next door would roar in the evenings and at night. Sometimes I lay awake worrying that they might break through the walls and come over.

Amrita and Rekha were four and two years old at the time and there were no playgrounds, parks, or play schools where they could meet other children. I too wanted companionship, so I invited my friend, Christine Weston to spend a month with us in Libya. As I described earlier, I had met Christine many years earlier during a memorable summer vacation with my family in Mussoorie. It was lovely having her visit, although the night-time lions' roars, which I had kept as a surprise from her, scared her out of her wits, just as it did me.

The big excitement during Christine's stay was the visit of UN Secretary General Dag Hammarskjold as the guest of King Idris. Since the king lived in a simple villa where he never entertained celebrities, all kinds of arrangements had to be made to ensure a western-style meal and entertainment for Hammarskjold. Sadly,

Amrita and Rekha

Libya's iron-clad rules of gender conduct meant that Christine and I couldn't even catch a glimpse of him, let alone greet him as I had hoped. Hammarskjold was the youngest secretary-general of the UN, and the only one who died while in office. He was killed in a plane crash two years after the Libya visit. He had been traveling to negotiate for peace during the crisis that had engulfed the Congo.

A week after the secretary-general's visit, we took a three-hour drive to Cyrene to see its famous Greek ruins. The drive through a landscape of desert sands on one side, and the ocean, on the other, was spectacular. Lending a touch of a bygone era were camels and camel herders plodding along the road. The ruins seemed completely abandoned, without even a fence or a guard to secure them and no signage or information boards to tell of their significance. We returned to Benghazi after a short walk around the hard to navigate site. Christine left for the U.S. a few days later and my daughters and I left a week after that for New Delhi.

After Romen finished his Libyan assignment, we returned to New York and soon settled into a comfortable groove. I returned to work and was soon engrossed with my job in the UN Human Rights Division. It was an interesting time to be living through. People from different countries and backgrounds were pouring into New York. The feminist movement was starting up, and I gravitated to it, wanting to better understand the nature and roots of discrimination women faced. Betty Friedan's classic, *The Feminine Mystique*, was to come out in 1963, but by the late 1950s she was already capturing through in-depth interviews the dissatisfaction of many women with their lives and status. Those insights would lay the basis for Friedan's famous depiction of "the problem with no name"—the sense of personal worthlessness that women had internalized from feeling like mere appendages of their husbands. To an extent, that reflected my personal life as well during my long periods of leave from my job.

To my delight, an unexpected vacancy at the UN in Delhi

enabled Romen to secure a two-year posting there. Typically, the UN Secretariat prohibited staff members from working in their country of origin. Papaji had built a beautiful two-story home with a swimming pool for us adjoining Mughal ruins in Hauz Khaz, then a rural area on the outskirts of Delhi. We would awaken to the sounds of peacocks on the lawn. The girls attended the Garden School, which was held on the spacious lawn of the principal, Mrs. Moitra. I spent lots of time with my parents and they delighted in getting to know their grand-daughters. I always felt complete confidence leaving the children in their care.

Meanwhile my family had moved from Hanuman Road, which had become a commercial center of Delhi surrounded by office buildings, to a beautiful home on a quiet, tree-lined street then called Ratendon Road. That two-floor home, with independent living units and luxurious, sprawling grounds, adjoined Lodhi Gardens—a large public park with monuments dating back to the 15th and 16th centuries. A scenic lake in the park is home to innumerable birds, including migratory ducks and geese which Park caretakers say have gotten so fat from unauthorized feedings by visitors that they can barely fly. Lodhi Gardens, with its colorful flowers and spacious grounds, are very popular with walkers, picnickers and children. It is a source of great pride to Delhi residents.

From our home, we could see back then some of the historical monuments in Lodi Gardens. Old spreading trees have partially hidden them now. It is as if the wonders and vistas beyond are being guarded from our eyes by these friendly sentinels.

My brother Patwant had moved back to Delhi from Bombay in 1962 and now lived upstairs above the original Lutyens-era bungalow on an additional floor designed by Patwant whose construction Papaji oversaw. My parents were delighted to have their son home again and living close by.

Romen received his last long overseas assignment to Thailand in 1963, and I found myself once again petitioning the UN for

Our garden at Amrita Sher-Gil Marg

unpaid leave. Romen had worked in Bangkok before I met him, so returning to Thailand was a little bit like coming home for him. He was most enthusiastic at the prospect of returning to his favorite city. He captured our girls' attention with his description of a modern city with canals full of boats, big and small, transporting children to school and adults to work. Small traders even conducted their commerce in the canals, selling products procured from aboard. To me Bangkok seemed to belong to an even earlier era, when boats were the main means of transportation.

Romen's enthusiasm was contagious, and I fell in love with Thailand almost immediately. I found Thai men and women gentle, laid-back and soft spoken. It was easy to adapt to Bangkok. Life was leisurely and it was a joy to shop at the markets. There were even floating markets on the water as well as those on land, selling fresh Thai, Indian and Chinese vegetables. The small wooden houses along the canals had beautiful orchids growing along the waterfront. The mighty Mekong river that flowed through the middle of the city was lined with temples, houses, and cottages. Vegetables and fruit that seemed exotic to us, such as durian—rather odorous but highly priced and prized by the Thais—pineapples, mangoes, mangosteen, and innumerable varieties of bananas. Presiding over the city was the Oriental Hotel, a splendorous landmark, with outdoor terrace tables laden with food for every palate.

Bangkok in the mid-sixties was a big, bustling, cosmopolitan city, with several multi-story buildings connected by overpasses and underpasses. The population included a large number of Chinese, Malays, Indians and Westerners. Cars, taxis, four-wheelers and six-wheelers, buses and scooters formed an unending vehicular river, and despite the well laid out roads and highways, Bangkok's famous traffic jams existed even in those days. The headquarters of the UN's Economic and Social Commission for Asia and the Pacific (now ESCAP) was located in Bangkok and its mandate had been expanded to include not only the economic but also social development for Asia and the Pacific. We found a charming little two-storied house on Soi 20, enclosed by a garden and a canal with its own orchid house, much to the delight of the children. It was not far from the International School Bangkok (ISB), where Amrita and Rekha were enrolled.

Before I could even settle down, I was offered a position at the ISB teaching English as a foreign language—a new subject at that time. This was a completely novel experience for me. I hadn't taught since my law school days in Delhi and had never tutored students that young. But I took up the assignment with enthusiasm and put together a program that was approved by the faculty.

My classroom consisted of students from kindergarten to 10th grade and this led to some piquant situations. Some of the students at the high school level were falling in love and the school's policy demanded all budding romances be discouraged. I remember two pairings particularly. One was a Swedish boy and a Japanese girl, the other an Italian boy and a Thai girl. The school was anxious about their amorous inclinations and asked me to handle the situation. I observed that the kids were perfectly well behaved. They sat on separate chairs and didn't hold hands in the classroom. Since no rules were broken, I believed no disciplinary action was required.

My students became very dependent on me since they couldn't communicate well with each other, or indeed with other students and teachers in the school. I remember one instance when I was laid up at home with a fever and two girls in their early teens walked several blocks and traffic crossings to look for me during their recess. Their teachers were frantic at their disappearance, until I called the school and assured them the girls were safe and would be dropped back shortly.

Amrita and Rekha were happy at school, making friends easily and perpetually excited about holidays. They were good children, attentive in the classroom and conscientious about homework. Amrita always took care of her younger sister. Romen was much less engaged with their scholastic progress than I was. But he loved to be with the family in his free time and was a "fun dad," who enjoyed doing out-of-the-box things together. Going to the market as a family every weekend was a major outing. He tried to teach the children Bengali, but with little success. Where he did succeed was to get them interested in food. He himself was adventurous about foreign cuisines and even came down once with hepatitis after eating a stew in the market place that he said was made of monkey brains.

On one occasion, Romen's work took him to Laos, Cambodia, and Vietnam, since he was in charge of the Mekong project which was promoting the economic development of the Mekong Delta. All three countries had been under French rule and each was crisscrossed by the Mekong River and its tributaries. We decided to make a 10-day family trip of it, which would become a high point of our Southeast Asia stay.

We first flew into Vientiane, the capital of the Laos People's Democratic Republic, on the majestic Mekong river. Laos is a landlocked country, surrounded by four countries—Burma and China to the northwest, Vietnam to the east, and Cambodia to the southwest. While the Laotians spoke in their own tongue, they also used French and most people knew a smattering of English. In Vientiane, we stayed in a big downtown hotel, with a large garden surrounded by high walls and a thick wire mesh to keep a bear in. Amrita and Rekha were fascinated by the animal and would follow it around. We were told that the bear belonged to the hotel. After a delicious dinner, we all went to bed. The next morning, we went down to visit the bear, but it was not to be seen anywhere. Upon further enquiry we learnt that he had been butchered the evening before and served to us for dinner. Unaware of what the meat course consisted of, we had found it very palatable. Learning about the sad fate of the bear was a source of much grief, especially for the children.

While Romen went to meetings, the children and I explored the local market in the central town square. There were beautiful silk batiks for women's sarongs, and colorful semiprecious stone necklaces. I was particularly enamored by the antique copper containers with beautifully engraved lids that Laotians used to store rice, beans and other dried goods. We also took walks on the river bank and did quick tours of the temples, although we did not make it to Luang Prabang, the ancient capital of Laos, with its renowned temples and other structures.

A couple of days later, we were on our way to Phnom Penh, the capital of Cambodia. Just a short flight from Vientiane, it was far grander and more built up than the city we had left, with a distinctly French air about it. Although it took us a day to reach, we made sure to visit the world's largest religious complex—the ruins of Angkor Wat, dating back to the 12th century.

The last remarkable country on this trip was Vietnam. Although the U.S. army was steadily building up its presence in the South, the Vietnam War had not yet broken out and it wasn't until 1965 that active U.S. combat units moved in. The North Vietnam we visited was known for being the home of Ho Chi Minh, the leader of the Vietnamese resistance movement. Hills and lakes marked the beautiful city of Hanoi, with the local population commuting by bicycles, rickshaws, or on foot. Ho Chi Minh's house, which was closed when we visited, looked very simple yet inspiring. As always, we visited the local market. New and mysterious foods always featured high in the family's priorities though only Romen was adventurous enough to sample some of the exotic meats. I stuck with vegetables of unknown origin, but they had to be cooked. The hot dumplings served up on street carts were mouth-watering.

The Vietnamese vendors, both men and women, struck us as very hardworking, buying and selling produce of all kinds and hawking consumer goods—always a big temptation for me. After a short coastal drive followed by a delicious French-Vietnamese dinner, it was time to return to Bangkok.

Soon after our return and after the annual school exams, Amrita came down with a serious case of hepatitis, which would lead to her having to miss the whole year of school. During that same period, I received a cable informing me that my beloved Maaji had passed away after a massive heart attack. Mamaji's death in 1962 at the young age of 60 was a great personal loss for me, but I always took solace from the fact that I had Maaji. She was my second mother. It was with her and Kabliji that I had made my first forays outside Delhi as a child. As soon as I heard the news, I flew to New Delhi, leaving the children in the care of their father and the household help. That stay was emotionally very fraught. After the funeral and the visits of friends and relatives were over, I found myself unable to do anything but crumple into a heap and cry my heart out.

But that season of personal tragedy was not yet over. Two

weeks later, Papaji had a heart attack. The cardiologist had barely reached home to see him when he passed away. I was filled once more with grief. With my parents and Maaji gone, I felt bereft of the love and guidance of family elders. Our home was emptied of occupants.

On top of those crushing losses, we were moving again in the winter of 1965. Life would never be the same. A few days after my father's funeral, Romen arrived from Bangkok with Amrita and Rekha and the four of us left Delhi for New York once again. An icy cold January morning greeted us when we landed in John F. Kennedy airport, and the weather reflected my grief.

five

MY UN HOME

The focus of this chapter shifts from family life to work, although the two have always been deeply inter-connected for me. It describes the most meaningful of my UN assignments, in the section on the status of women and in the branch on Palestine.

Feminism had always been close to my heart and I brought to my work not only my legal background but my lifelong personal experiences. As my daughters were now growing up, I could take them with me to international conferences. Doing so proved to be formative for them both. Amrita joined me at the global women's conferences in Mexico City, Copenhagen, and Nairobi and later wrote scholarly analyses of them. Rekha came with me to a preparatory conference in Nicaragua and the Mexico City conference. Her journalistic writing has been deeply informed by her exposure to global women's struggles for equality.

The UN created the Commission on the Status of Women (CSW) as a part of the Human Rights Division in 1946. The CSW is the principal global intergovernmental organization that is exclusively dedicated to advancing gender equality. It has played an instrumental role in documenting women's education, employment, inheritance, and legal status, and shaping global norms and laws to promote women's rights. In 1967 the CSW persuaded the UN General Assembly to adopt the Declaration on the Elimination of Discrimination Against Women (DEDAW), a legally binding Convention that was a precursor to the historic Convention on the Elimination of all Forms of Discrimination Against Women (CEDAW) which became known as the international women's bill of rights.

The idea for international women's year took root in 1973. Behind the official decisions was the grass roots activism of women at the UN Secretariat. I recall meeting for coffee with a few junior staff members from the Secretariat in the Delegates lounge and suggesting that a year devoted to women's rights would be a logical sequel to the UN's declaration of 1973 as the year of population control and 1974 as the year of development. Our dreams came true when the Branch supported us. The UN proclaimed 1975 as International Women's Year and selected Helvi Sipilä to be Assistant Secretary General for Social Development and Humanitarian Affairs.

To my great surprise and delight, I was assigned the task of preparing the draft World Plan of Action. It was an overwhelming assignment that had to be carried out in a short period of time. My first objective was to gain insight into policies, plans, deficiencies and achievements of national governments with respect to women's rights. The second was to understand the procedures we had to follow and the means by which we could gain the assent, first of the UN, and then of national governments. After drafting the Plan, I had to submit it for approval to my supervisor, Margaret (Molly) Bruce, and other senior members of the Branch. These senior staff members then sent it to the relevant UN offices and departments, including the Secretary General's Office, the Division of Human Rights, Social Development, and Population and specialized UN agencies like UNESCO, WHO, FAO, UNICEF, and ILO. It would then have to be finalized by the CSW. National governments organized regional conferences throughout the world to consider the draft plan and draw up their own priorities based on the UN document. The focal point of the year was to be the first UN World Conference on Women in Mexico City in 1975.

March 3, 1975, preparatory conference for Mexico City;
Helvi Sipilä, Molly Bruce, and me.

One hundred and thirty-three delegates, the majority of them women, attended the Mexico City conference. This in itself was a landmark event, although delegates were obliged to represent the positions of their national governments and not voice their own views. Inevitably, many women who attended were relatives of male politicians. But there were some important exceptions, like Cosmonaut Valentina Tereshkova, a factory worker and amateur sky-diver who was inducted into the Soviet Air Force and was the first woman to go to space. Some female relatives departed from their prescribed roles. For example, Ashraf Pahlavi from Iran carved out a distinctive identity, independent of her brother, the controversial Shah, by raising funds for the conference,

Equally remarkable was the Tribune, a parallel meeting of NGOs, which 6,000 women attended. It established a key role for feminist civil society organizations in keeping national governments and international organizations accountable. The Tribune was held simultaneously, but at some distance from the official conference in Mexico City. It provided an arena for lively, open-ended discussions on the requisites for women's empowerment. In addition to thirty-six planned meetings, the Tribune hosted 200 spontaneously organized sessions. Participants explored questions concerning sexual orientation, the rights of indigenous women, and gender violence, topics that were muted or absent from the official conference. Geo-political differences surfaced here as well, particularly along North-South lines. The sharpest divide was between feminists from the global North, who emphasized the importance of sexual and reproductive rights, and women from the global South, who prioritized socio-economic development and criticized the impact of Western imperialism on their countries. Still, the Tribune agreed on proposed amendments to the Plan and agreed that the UN should take more steps to ensure its implementation by creating standing bodies to monitor progress. The UN subsequently created the International Research and Training Institute for the Advancement of Women (INSTRAW) and the United Nations Development Fund for Women (UNIFEM). The Tribune also urged the UN to improve policies for hiring and promoting women officials.

I was also delighted that the UN agreed to my suggestion that we hold a "Journalists Encounter." The journalists captured media attention with daily bulletins on the deliberations at both the Tribune and the official conference.

In recent years there has been a great deal of debate about the value of UN conferences. They have been criticized as overly expensive, bureaucratic, and ultimately ineffective. But having been so closely associated with the genesis and development of these conferences, my own assessment is much more positive. True, there were times that I was frustrated by having to speak in the name of the UN Secretariat and not openly express my own views in public forums. True, the process of change was slow and unwieldy. However, the difficulties of organizing this conference cannot be overstated. Cold War tensions dominated international politics and meant that the U.S. and Soviet Union paid scant attention to women's rights. When they did so, they approached them from very different angles—the U.S. with a focus on civil and political rights and the Soviet Union with a focus on economic rights. And yet, by revealing the extent and pervasiveness of gender inequality, the global conferences served to politicize those who had not previously taken the issue seriously. For all the contentious debates that took place both at the Tribune and at the official conference, women had a unique opportunity for deliberation and debate in a truly international setting.

My legal background and years of experience working for the UN made me appreciate the importance of negotiating and preventing polarization. Some of this entailed behind the scenes conversations with the official delegates, to persuade them to modify their stance before they participated in the official meetings. I had often attended meetings of the General Assembly and gotten to know the younger national delegates. We formed an informal network which enabled us to consult with one another and decide how we could best influence official policies. I knew that delegates had to consult with their national governments and lacked the authority to act autonomously, even if they privately agreed with us. If we could not persuade delegates to support the Plan, we encouraged them to abstain rather than voting negatively. I also learned the importance of linguistic subtlety and engaged in endless revisions of draft documents until everyone could agree upon the final version.

The Mexico City conference adopted the 1975 World Plan of Action (WPA) and declared 1975-1985 the decade for women. It called upon all development organizations and specialized allies to make a concerted effort to equalize women's status in their areas of competence, namely, education, vocational training, employment, food production, health, nutrition, social services, and reproductive rights. It emphasized the potential roles the media, NGOs, and scholars could play and the need for legislative and administrative action. The conference recognized women as equal partners in development rather than passive victims and beneficiaries.

The conference not only encouraged member countries to develop policies which would lead to the improvement of women's lives but also mapped out a series of follow-up conferences. The second global mid-decade conference would be held in Copenhagen in 1980 and the third in Nairobi in 1985. Between the 1975 and the 1980 conferences, the UN organized regional conferences throughout the world. Argentina hosted the Latin American and Caribbean Conference in 1976. President Isabel Martinez de Peron, the third wife of President Juan Peron, was scheduled to inaugurate the conference. The evening before the opening, Helvi Sipilä hosted a reception for Isabel Peron and the regional delegations. She praised the president for inviting the UN to hold the event in Argentina.

I woke up early the next morning to check on the conference arrangements but to my surprise I found the main boulevard lined with military tanks and armed guards. A little later, I received a call from Helvi informing me there had been a coup. Isabel Peron had been deposed and was under house arrest. The seminar was cancelled. A car with an escort was sent to take me to the hotel rooms of all the delegates and UN senior staff and inform them.

World events again interfered when the second global women's conference was approaching in 1980. It was supposed to be held in Iran but in the wake of the overthrow of the Shah, the Iranian Revolution and the hostage crisis, the conference had to be moved to Copenhagen instead. It was held in July 1980. The major goal of the conference was to provide a mid-decade assessment of progress in implementing the goals established by the World Plan of Action at the 1975 conference. Its most significant achievement was the formal signing of CEDAW. It explicitly defined discrimination against women and set up an agenda for national action to end it. It targeted culture and tradition as significant forces in shaping gender roles and family relations. And it was the first human rights treaty to affirm women's reproductive rights.

One hundred forty-five states, with around 1,500 delegates, participated in the official conference, which was presided over by Lise Østergaard, Cultural Minister of Denmark. Lucille Mair, a distinguished foreign service veteran from Jamaica was the Secretary-General of the conference and the first Under-Secretary General in UN history. She was an inspiring leader, and together she and I pushed back against the Western feminist perspective that many Secretariat members promoted. We insisted that the UN had to broaden its vision to address the conditions of the most severely oppressed women and that we could not do so without addressing geo-political inequalities.

One of my most important goals for this conference was to address the conditions of Palestinian and South African women. The U.S. at that point had a good diplomatic relationship with South Africa's apartheid regime. However, in the wake of the Soweto uprising of 1976 and the death of Steven Biko in jail in 1977, American public opinion was shifting toward supporting anti-apartheid efforts. We wanted to push the UN to give not only humanitarian and educational aid, but also to help in the struggle to end apartheid and create an independent Palestinian state. I hired two scholars in 1979 to assist me in this effort. The first was Richard Lapchik, who had written a Ph.D. dissertation on the apartheid regime, taught African politics and become the American leader of a very successful sports boycott of South Africa. When I interviewed Rich for the position, I told him, "you're the wrong race, the wrong sex, and the wrong nationality, but you're perfect for the job." I hired him anyway. The second was Stephanie Urdang, whom I met through Rich. Stephanie was an anti-apartheid activist and scholar who had done extensive research on South African women's activism against the apartheid regime. She provided links to women leaders in South Africa who had fought for many generations against apartheid.

As we were heading toward Copenhagen, Zimbabwe became independent and we managed to get Sally Mugabe, the new first lady of an independent Zimbabwe, to be a featured speaker at the conference. I remember the joy in the hall that accompanied her presence as it became apparent that the shackles of colonialism in the remaining strongholds of racism might be smashed sooner than we thought.

The Copenhagen conference was rife with geo-political divides which were even more far-reaching than those at the Mexico City conference. A number of NGOs drew attention to the situation of women and children in South Africa and the urgency of UN action. In addition, the UN Centre against Apartheid prepared reports on women under apartheid and recommended a series of measures to assist Namibian and South African women. These were endorsed by the General Assembly. The UN also addressed the plight of Palestinian women. As a result, South Africa boycotted the conference and the U.S. refused to endorse any policies which criticized Zionism. North-South conflicts also became more pronounced.

The parallel Tribune was even more lively and politically fraught. As in Mexico City, the members of the Forum continued the tradition of presenting their additions to the Program of Action at the official session. A group of women led by the Bolivian activist Domitila Barrios de Chungara was barred by the police from entering the plenary meeting. Tensions only abated after Lucille Mair wisely decided to meet with the group and allowed them to present their recommendations. Some of the tensions at the Forum reflected the emergence of multiple understandings of the relationship between feminism and nationalism in the global South. Among the participants were Iranian women, who considered the use of the hijab a symbol of anti-colonial struggle, alongside Egyptian feminists like Nawal el Saadawi, who opposed the practice of veiling.

And yet we could claim some significant achievements. The

Program of Action that was adopted called for nations to take stronger measures to ensure women's ownership and control of property, as well as women's rights with respect to inheritance, child custody and loss of nationality. The Program expanded on the previous targets to improve women's status and decided on a follow-up conference at the end of the decade.

In 1985, Kenya hosted the World Conference to Review and Appraise the Achievements of the United Nations Decade for Women: Equality, Development and Peace. The Nairobi conference mandate was to establish concrete measures to overcome obstacles to achieving the Decade's goals. Participants included 1,900 delegates from 157 member states; a parallel NGO Forum attracted around 12,000 civil society participants. It was an exciting time to participate in the Nairobi conference. Because of the conference location, it was well attended by African women and representation from the global South was larger than ever. The event was described by many as "the birth of global feminism."

By the third conference in Nairobi in 1985, I had retired from the UN. However, I attended the NGO Forum as a member of Development Alternatives with Women for a New Era (DAWN), an India-based organization of women in the global South. DAWN was created in Bangalore, India in August 1984, in part to prepare for the Nairobi conference. It presented a critique of global forces that impacted poor women in the global South and presented an alternative vision, putting macro-economic global issues on the feminist agenda. Working with a truly remarkable group of women, including Devaki Jain, who formed DAWN, I came to appreciate how powerful movements for women's empowerment were in Asia, Africa and Latin America.

Realizing that the goals of the Mexico City Conference had not been adequately met, the 157 participating governments adopted the Nairobi Forward-looking Strategies for the Advancement of Women which outlined measures for achieving gender equality at the national level and for promoting women's participation in peace and development efforts. The document broke new ground by declaring all issues to be women's issues. By the end of the UN Decade for Women, 127 member states had established institutions to promote policy, research and programs aimed at women's advancement and participation in development.

However, sad to say, many governments failed to maintain their commitments and the UN lacked the means of enforcement to rectify this. By 2014, a record 143 countries guaranteed equality between men and women in their Constitutions. Yet 52 countries had not taken this step. And even in countries that provide legal guarantees of gender equality, gender disparities in economic, social and political realms remain stark. On average, women in the labor market still earn 24% less than men globally. Despite the General Assembly "Declaration on the Elimination of Violence against Women," sexual violence is alarmingly pervasive throughout the world. As of August 2015, only 22% of all national parliamentarians were women, double the 11.3 percent in 1995, but still woefully inadequate. It is ironic that women are also under-represented in managerial and decision-making positions within the UN Secretariat despite five-year Action Plans, including Strategic Plans to achieve Gender Equality in the representation of women at the D1 (starting director's) level. At the current rate of progress, it is estimated that it will not be until the year 2120 when equality is achieved.

UN Conference on Question of Palestine, Geneva, August— September 1983

UN Secretary General Perez de Cuellar appointed Lucille as the Secretary General of the Conference on the Question of Palestine. I respected Lucille's experience working with Nelson Mandela and the non-aligned bloc and was delighted when she asked me to take up a challenging assignment as the director of her office. My colleagues and I had been complaining that women were only allotted "soft subjects." Now we had the opportunity to take up tough political issues. Was I prepared for it? I had no doubt that I was.

To assist me in this daunting task, I sought out the assistance of three brilliant people. Rich Lapchik, who had proved invaluable in Nairobi, was one of them. The second was Rich's best friend from graduate school, Donald Betz, who was both a deeply informed scholar and a committed activist on behalf of Palestinians. And the third was the legendary scholar and activist, Edward Said. I had invited him to one of the scheduled events of the Palestinian Conference. Of course, I had obtained authorization from the UN Secretary General's Chef de Cabinet, who had cleared it with the Secretary General. However, there was consternation within the UN that I had potentially embarrassed the Secretary General by inviting such a controversial figure. Fortunately, the Secretary General was charmed by Edward and appreciated Edward's statesmanlike approach and wisdom. He saw that Edward's membership in the Palestine National Council elevated its level of discussion. Edward attended the UN Conference although his health was failing.

Save for the Cold War, there was no more controversial subject internationally than Palestine. The conference organized five regional meetings prior to the international meeting in Geneva. Most countries of the world supported an independent Palestinian state, but this was not the case in Europe, the U.S., or Israel. By the time we got to Geneva, it appeared that every nation except the United States and Israel was ready to acknowledge an independent Palestinian state. At the same time, the Palestine Liberation Organization (PLO) was moving toward recognition of Israel's right to exist. I left Geneva feeling hopeful for the first time on this critical issue. However, tragically, hundreds of Palestinian civilians—men, women and children—were brutally massacred at the refugee camps of Sabra and Shatila in West Beirut on 17 and 18 September 1982. It cast a dark cloud on the ensuing meetings.

Five regional preparatory meetings for the Conference were held from March to July 1983. The African regional meeting that took place in Arusha, Tanzania, concentrated on the political and jurisdictional aspects of the question of Palestine. The Latin American meeting, held in Managua, Nicaragua, examined the legal aspects of the Palestine question and affirmed the Palestinian right to their own state. The Palestinians' socio-economic conditions and the status of Jerusalem were the agenda items of the West Asian Regional Preparatory Meeting, which was held in Sharjah, United Arab Emirates. A careful analysis of the economic viability of a Palestinian state was prepared by our staff for that meeting. The strategic and geopolitical aspects of the Palestine issue were examined at the Asian regional meeting in Kuala Lumpur, Malaysia. It was attended by 40 States and 16 foreign ministers, which amply demonstrated the interest of the Asian region in resolving this issue. The Kuala Lumpur recommendations called for the formation of an independent and sovereign Palestinian state. Reports of the five regional preparatory meetings and the UN Conference on the Question of Palestine (CQP) recommendations were put before the Conference.

The CQP took place in Geneva, August-September 1983. The Conference was opened by UN Secretary General Perez de Cuellar. Massambe Sarre of Senegal was elected Chairman. The Conference was attended by 117 states, along with 20 states that had observer status, and the PLO. The twenty state observers were from Western European countries, as well as Australia, Canada, Guatemala, Honduras, Japan, and New Zealand. Israel, the U.S. and several other countries opposed holding the Conference.

Since Lucille Mair was unable to attend the conference, I spoke in her place. Some excerpts from my speech are as follows:

> ...the United Nations' responsibility for resolving the question of Palestine is unmistakable, imperative and urgent...

UN meeting with Yasser Arafat, former chair of the PLO

The objectives of this Conference, as most participants are doubtless aware, are to increase international awareness of the issues and to seek more effec-
tive ways and means of ensuring the achievement of
Palestinian rights. The importance and timeliness of
these efforts have been heightened sharply by the war
in Lebanon and the massacres of Sabra and Shatila as
well as the continually deteriorating situation in the
West Bank and Gaza.

I referred to the recommendations that had emerged from the
Kuala Lumpur conference, which went beyond appeals for Security Council action to maintain peace and security in the Middle
East. They strongly urged the establishment of appropriate insti-
tutional arrangements "for the actual formation of an independent and sovereign state to be governed by and for the Palestinian
people." I said,

Since we came into existence as a Conference secretariat seven months back, we feel that significant

progress has been made in raising levels of public understanding and formulating recommendation for action in these regional meetings. However, it would be naive to minimize the difficulties that lie ahead and the work that still needs to be done, for which no effort is too great. Seminars like this are invaluable towards that effort. Not only will a solution to the question of Palestine bring justice where justice is long overdue for the 4.5 million Palestinian people, and peace to a region which has been fraught with wars, but it will amount to a restoration of faith in the United Nations and the principles of the Charter upon which it was founded.

The Conference adopted a "Declaration on Palestine" and approved a "Program of Action for the Achievement of Palestinian Rights." It addressed the need for a comprehensive, just and lasting political settlement based on UN resolutions of the inalienable rights of Palestinian people. Those included their rights to self-determination, to establish their own independent state, and the right of PLO representatives to participate on equal footing with other parties. It opposed all Israeli legislative and administrative measures that altered the character and status of the holy city of Jerusalem and made Jerusalem the capital of Israel. The Conference mandated that the UN convene an international peace conference on the Middle East with participation on equal footing of all parties to the Arab-Israeli conflict, including the PLO.

My work on women's rights and Palestinian self-determination persuaded me of the need for global attention to oppressed and marginalized groups whose interests were often overlooked by nation states. For all its flaws and failures, and all the attempts of member nations to undermine it, the UN provided a unique forum for addressing these issues. And yet I'm also painfully

aware of how much work remains to be done to achieve the emancipation of both women and of Palestine. I miss those who could
have illuminated the path forward. Above all, I miss Edward Said,
who battled leukemia until 2003. With his passing, the world lost
a voice of reason, wisdom and compassion at a time that was most
needed. He would have been horrified to see how badly the situation of Palestinians has deteriorated since his lifetime.

six

MY LITTLE WORLDS IN NEW YORK AND WOODSTOCK

O ur first home in New York was in East Harlem, long before the area became gentrified. There were few racially integrated apartment buildings; 1270 Fifth Avenue, where we lived, was an exception, and Romen and I were committed to living in a multiracial environment. Although it was a long trek from there to the UN, we loved the neighborhood that adjoined Central Park. We made good friends with several neighbors, including Lloyd Barnes, a physician, who became our family doctor, his wife Winnie, and their daughters. We later moved to an apartment at 345 East 69th Street, on the upper East Side. It was conveniently located within walking distance to the UN as well as to the UN International School, which Amrita and Rekha entered, in seventh and fifth grades respectively. Romen joined the school board.

The '60's were an exciting and turbulent time to be living in New York with teenage daughters. The anti-war activism, civil rights protests and burgeoning feminism offered a visceral living-history lesson. The assassinations of John F. Kennedy and Martin Luther King had a profound effect on us. Young people were burning their draft cards and marching against the anti-Communist fervor that drove U.S. involvement in Vietnam. Others were escaping into a fog of substances, from pot to heroin.

Although we fully supported student activism, as foreigners on

On the rooftop of our apartment at 69ᵗʰ Street

UN visas we had to walk a fine line with respect to our family's political involvement. Both girls had become radicalized and felt strongly about social justice causes. But their school cautioned international students against participating in moratoriums or other anti-war events because we were officially guests of the US government. We were simultaneously political dissenters and outsiders who were barred from fully participating.

The free-love era and its relaxed attitudes toward drug use caused Romen a great deal of consternation. Although he was progressive on many issues, he was a traditional father who was not above heading out in his pajamas and raincoat if the girls were not home by the agreed-upon time. I tried to calm him down with reassurances that they were responsible kids. But his upbringing made it hard for him to adjust to these new norms.

Amrita was unusually responsible from an early age. She was not only protective of her younger sister and considerate of me (taking on cooking and household chores from an early age) but also a serious student who set high goals for herself. Rekha was more fun loving. She aspired to be an actress, and at one point wanted to drop out of school to devote herself to a full-time acting career. We persuaded her to settle for weekend acting classes at the American Academy of Dramatic Arts.

With Rekha, Romen, and Amrita in NY in the '70s

For years, we thought about getting a place in the country to escape for weekends from the high rises of Manhattan. Our daughters' school had no outdoor area for sports or recreation. Romen wanted to write poems and novels on a deck of his own. He loved being surrounded by nature and I wanted to get my hands dirty and grow flowers and shrubs.

Bertie and Oden Meeker, dear friends from New Delhi, where Oden had been posted as director of Cooperative for American Relief Everywhere (CARE), invited us to spend weekends with them in their home in Woodstock, New York. It was a two-hour drive from New York City, with lovely mountains and the Ashokan reservoir—quite unlike the suburban towns with their cookie-cutter housing complexes. Bertie was a very good artist and Oden authored several books, including *The Little World of Laos*, and articles for The New Yorker. Their friend Peter Whitehead had a number of villas on a mountain near the village, which he rented out to artists and other creative types. His father, Ralph Whitehead, from England was an original settler in Byrdcliffe and had attracted artists, musicians, and theatre people. He founded the Byrdcliffe Theater. There was an 18-hole golf course and club and a number of small charming restaurants with Italian, French, Chinese, and even Indian cuisines. Woodstock became famous for the legendary 1969 music festival bearing its name that featured three days of peace, love, and rock and roll. Ironically, it didn't actually take place in Woodstock but rather in Bethel, NY, about an hour's drive away, on 600 acres of land owned by Max Yasgur, a dairy farmer. More than half a million people attended what is still considered the ultimate counter culture event of the 1960s.

Thanks to our weekend home in Woodstock in the '70s, we had access to an artsy Bohemian community in the heart of the Catskill Forest Preserve. For a town of its size, it was awash in music venues and art galleries, and home to some famed rock and roll musicians. Bob Dylan and The Band were frequently spotted in the area. It also had a beautiful Buddhist monastery, a playhouse, and a Saturday farmers' market.

In some respects, Woodstock resembled the mountainous retreats in the Himalayas known as hill stations created by the British Raj. They were reasonably close to the plains but offered a respite from the summer heat. During our summer vacations, my parents, Patwant and I used to take the train up to Simla or Mussoorie. They were a comfortable distance from steaming Delhi. Unfortunately, our daughters and grandsons had not grown up near such hill stations, but Woodstock provided an attractive alternative.

After spending weekends with the Meekers, I was increasingly interested in getting a home in Woodstock. We weren't exactly floating in cash, as we had two daughters in private schools, but we lived comfortably. Woodstock was very close to Romen's heart, and somehow he could never entertain the idea of renting a house to test it out first. When he saw a house he loved, he felt compelled to buy it. This was how he purchased a house that was very well located, not far from the center of town. It had a couple of acres of

Our home in Woodstock

land, a stream running through it, two charming living areas for sitting, drinking and eating, and a beautiful terrace. However, the house itself was architecturally uninteresting. It was a two-story standard box structure that could have been located in one of the boroughs of NYC or a modest house in suburbia.

Romen asked me how I liked the house. I was uncertain but assured him it had great potential. He said that I could tear it down and rebuild it according to my wishes. I agreed. I was lucky to find a very nice builder with good aesthetic sensibilities. We opened up the front wall, moved the tiny fireplace to a nice open one in the corner, and enlarged the tiny counter from the kitchen to the dining area. We put in a cathedral ceiling and a staircase with window boxes. The sun shone and the flowers blossomed. The house became beautiful.

With Romen

We spent many happy weekends there with our daughters and close friends. Romen's creative spirit soared; it was the launchpad for several of his books. Woodstock became our favorite spot for special celebrations like Thanksgiving and Christmas. Romen took charge. He usually took time off from work to head up early to buy ingredients for his lavish gourmet adventures. Our very close friends, Dick and Lucy Manoff, and their sons, partners and children all joined us, along with Amrita, Rekha, and their friends.

Relaxing in Woodstock

The hunting season would be open for a short period every fall and Romen always preferred a wild bird to one from a supermarket. One year's "super-duper wing ding Thanksgiving dinner" turned out to be a total surprise. Romen decided to go hunting for turkey, which he planned to serve to our house full of guests. Fearing that he might come back empty-handed, I bought some fancy appetizers—oysters, snails, pates, and cheeses. Time passed.

My guests and I ate and drank—but there was no sign of the chef or the turkey. Finally, Romen's feeble voice on the phone informed me that there was some trouble on his end, but it would soon be sorted out.

It turned out that Romen had lost his sense of direction and landed up in the neighboring small town of Phoenicia, in front of a housing complex. He spotted a bird flying high in the sky behind the trees and shot it down. Alas it was not a wild turkey but a woman's pet pigeon, with a nametag on its foot. The woman was hysterical and called the police, who arrested Romen. Neither she nor the police officer were moved by Romen's claims that he was a diplomat. The police officer took him into the station and said he would have to call Washington, D.C. to determine Romen's status. The cop allowed Romen to make just one phone call. He called his friend Harry Kennedy, who arrived and promptly paid the bail. The policeman was keen to get home to his Thanksgiving dinner but had to await a call back from a higher authority. Finally, success. The voice at the other end, an official in Washington, asked

Rekha, Romen, me and Amrita

whether Romen was being cooperative. Upon getting a positive response, he advised releasing him, after compensating the lady for her pigeon and mental anguish.

Romen and I would retire from the UN when we turned 60 (the mandatory retirement age at the UN). We soon returned to India to live. But before we left, we had the joy of seeing our daughter Amrita marry Mark Kesselman on July 7, 1984. Mark was a professor in Political Science in Columbia University.

Amrita had graduated with honors from Cornell University and got her doctorate in political science from Columbia. She obtained a teaching position at Amherst College. It gave me great satisfaction that despite growing up mostly outside India, her research focused on India. Rekha decided on a journalism career and has spent of her professional life as an opinion columnist for the Des Moines Register. Both our daughters married men who shared their professional interests.

Amrita and Mark's wedding took place in Opus 40 in Woodstock. It was a beautiful site, originally a stone quarry which Harvey Fite, a sculptor, had bought. Inspired by the Mexican pyramids, he had planned to build a few pyramids on the property, using the stone from the abandoned quarry. He also planned to organize lakes, amidst the beautiful landscaping that he designed. After spending many years on the project, and nearly completing his dream, he tragically died in 1982, as a result of falling from his tractor. The project remained incomplete. But it was still spectacular.

Amrita's husband Mark was a non-observant Jew, Amrita's father Romen was a non-observant Hindu and I'm a Sikh. The marriage ceremony was secular but drew on our different cultural traditions. It was held, as is customary in Jewish ceremonies, under a "chuppah." Their friend, Kris Glen, a judge on the New York State Supreme Court, who was known as "the red judge" because of her leftist views, officiated. I suspect that some of our friends were shocked by her radical speech!

Mark and Amrita at their wedding

There was a classical Indian dance after the ceremony in the "Bharat Natyam" style by Indrani Rahman, a very celebrated and famous Indian dancer and dear friend, and by Indrani's daughter Sukanya. It was followed by Indian classical sitar music. Then came drinks and hors d'oeuvres followed by an Indian dinner with toasts and speeches to the couple. The 130 guests included friends from Amherst College, Columbia University, members of the UN Secretariat, and many relatives. It was a beautiful and memorable wedding. The stage and setting were exquisite.

Amrita's wedding: Becca Dreyfus (Mark's niece), me, Mark, Judy Kesselman (Mark's sister), Rekha, Kris Glen (judge), Amrita, Romen, and Ann Kesselman (Mark's mother)

Rekha moved to Woodstock full-time in 1982, after getting a Master's degree from the Columbia School of Journalism. She got a job as a reporter at a local newspaper, The Kingston Daily Freeman. A year after Amrita's marriage, Rekha wed Rob Borsellino, the editor at the Freeman. It would have been tough matching the splendor of Opus 40 but Rekha wanted a simple ceremony and reception on the lawn of our Woodstock house. We decided to use the money we saved by not renting Opus 40 to extend the lawn of our house to accommodate a large party. I hung colorful saris from the tall fir trees. They looked very festive and added an Indian ambience. They also ended up staying there: it was too hard to get them down.

Rekha's wedding was homespun. Rob was Catholic so there were readings from the Bible, the Sikh and Hindu holy books, after which they were married by a judge. They garlanded each other with fresh flowers to the accompaniment of live sitar music. It was a magical moment. The dinner was a resplendent meal. The bride and groom then drove off in a big grand second-hand car after the champagne toasts and dancing.

Rob and Rekha at their wedding with Amrita officiating

Rekha's wedding: Jo Borsellino (Rob's mother), Romen, Rob,
Rekha, me, Amrita, and Mark

A few days later they left for their honeymoon at Trevignano, Italy, a charming fishing village on Lake Bracciano, where we had bought an apartment. About an hour's drive from Rome, it was an old town with narrow cobblestone streets and stone houses. Our apartment was on the waterfront with lots of boating and sailing and fishing and charming restaurants on the lake front. Interestingly this was Rob's first visit to Italy—the land of his forefathers and foremothers—which Rekha introduced him to.

Their honeymoon was cut short because the paper for which Rekha worked flew her to Bombay to pursue an investigation of two young American men who were involved in smuggling gold into India and got arrested.

Some time after their American weddings, Amrita and Mark, and Rekha and Rob, returned to India for wedding festivities at the extended family home in Calcutta.

Amrita's Calcutta wedding: Romen, Mark, Amrita and me

*Rekha's Calcutta wedding: Romen, Rob, Mira Sett (our niece),
Rekha, me, and Romen's maasi (aunt)*

Six years later, Rekha got a job as an editorial writer with the Des Moines Register, a significant step up in the world of journalism. She moved with her younger son, Romen, to Des Moines, leaving her older son, Raj, with Rob. Rob was a real trooper. He took care of Raj and after nearly a year, quit his job and moved to Des Moines, uncertain where he would work. He was eventually offered a job at the Register and both he and Rekha ultimately became columnists for the Register. They had very distinctive styles and interests.

I became far closer to my sons-in-law, Mark and Rob, than I would ever have imagined. I developed easy-going bantering relationships with them both, premised on love, trust, shared values, and mutual respect.

With Rob in Des Moines

With Mark at the Delhi Golf Club

And then there were my precious grandsons: Raj and Romen (the sons of Rob and Rekha) and Ishan and Javed (the sons of Amrita and Mark). Having raised two daughters, I was apprehensive about grandsons. All my stereotypes about girls being more loving and caring than boys were put to rest by my playful, funny, thoughtful grandsons.

With Raj in Albany, NY

Javed, me, and Ishan in Peekskill, NY

Rekha, Raj, Ishan and me in Normandy, France

With Mark, Amrita, Ishan, Rob, and Raj in Normandy

Rekha, Romen, Raj, and me

Raj, Rob, Romen, and me in Rome

Javed, Ishan, and me in Amherst

Romen, Rob, Amrita, Ishan, Javed, me, and Rekha in Amherst

Romen, Romen, Raj, and me at our Delhi home

Romen, me, and Raj in our NY apartment

With Ishan at our NY apartment

With Raj

seven

TRAGIC HOMECOMING

R omen and I retired from the UN at the mandatory age of sixty, in 1983. He retired on October 10th, and I retired the following day. We always planned to return to India after retiring, although he was more reluctant than me to give up our home in NY. The big question was which city would we return to—his home in Calcutta or mine in New Delhi? We finally decided in favor of New Delhi, where I had inherited our big beautiful house and garden on Amrita Sher-Gil Marg.

After a lifetime in the United States, returning to India was both exciting and intimidating. Having spent thirty-five years in a career at the UN, I knew no other. I felt very confident about my understanding of the issues and procedures at the UN. I had the support of a strong network of friends and colleagues there. I didn't feel ready to retire from work when I was so full of energy and ambition, but I knew that I would have to refashion myself in India. My secretary at the UN asked me several times if I hadn't gotten my age wrong. How I wished I had.

We went to Delhi in mid-October 1984 and stayed upstairs with my brother Patwant while I got my part of the house, the downstairs half, painted and furnished. Patwant had become a major public intellectual and since 1984, a spokesperson for the Sikh community. His interests had shifted from urban design to global politics to Sikhism and the Punjab, and he published

At the UN

several books on the subject. I was inspired by his courageous willingness to speak truth to power and grateful to him for easing my transition back to Delhi. Amrita and Mark, who were on sabbatical, joined us there. Days after my arrival, a tragedy unfolded that was to forever mark my homecoming. On October 31, 1984, one of Prime Minister Indira Gandhi's two Sikh security guards shot Gandhi as she was leaving her house. She was rushed to the All India Institute of Medical Sciences, but could not be saved. Her assassin was enraged by Gandhi's actions in the Punjab.

By way of background, in the first week of June 1984, Gandhi had ordered "Operation Blue Star," which entailed the army moving into the Golden Temple compound and storming the Akal Takht, a beautiful white marble shrine within the compound, destroying the marble pavements and walk ways. The library in the Akal Takht containing invaluable handwritten manuscripts, some by the Sikh gurus, were burned. The timing of the military attack, June 1-8, 1984, was cruel. June 5th is a very holy day for the Sikhs because it was the day the fifth Sikh Guru was martyred. Thousands of Sikhs had come to the Golden Temple to commemorate the occasion. I felt shock and outrage by the attack on our most sacred shrine and shattered by memories of our annual family visits to the Golden Temple during my childhood.

The Army claimed that 500 Sikh militants and 83 Army personnel were killed in the attacks. Most independent sources believe that the casualties were much higher, and that the army killed thousands of civilians when it attacked the Golden Temple. Was this a declaration of war by the government on the Sikh community?

The day that Mrs. Gandhi was assassinated, groups of Hindus who blamed Sikhs for her murder, attacked 42 *gurdwaras* throughout Delhi and butchered 2,000 Sikhs in the city. The next four days witnessed the worst carnage since the 1947 Partition of India. These were not riots but organized violence against the Sikhs, with the connivance of the ruling Congress party, the Delhi Administration and the police. Thousands of families lost everything: their relatives, homes, possessions, and food supplies. According to one estimate, the number of refugees was 50,000. The survivors of the holocaust were left horror struck and in a state of disbelief. Children who had witnessed rape and murder were traumatized.

From my brother's apartment, on the second floor of our home, we could see dense smoke. The city was in flames. An angry mob tried to enter our home and was deterred by our servants. Although our neighbors encouraged us to leave, we refused. The damage was far greater in poor neighborhoods like Trilokpuri and Mongolpuri, on the outskirts of Delhi.

Once the violence had abated, we drove through Delhi and saw buildings in which the apartments inhabited by Sikhs were gutted while those occupied by Hindus were untouched. We later learned that municipal officials gave the mobs voter registration lists indicating which apartments were occupied by Sikhs.

Like millions of other Sikhs, I was heartbroken by Mrs. Gandhi's assassination, yet our grief was not recognized. All Sikhs became suspect, as if the entire Sikh community was responsible for her death. The poignancy of the situation did not escape me. I had always found solace and pride in my Sikh identity. I had two homes in India, one in Delhi, and the other in Amritsar, which I had visited every summer as a child. But the Sikhs were now being massacred in both places and neither home felt safe anymore. I shared the grief and sorrow that all Sikhs experienced as they saw their places of worship desecrated and their community members brutalized. I was also horrified by what India had become since the time I had first left and moved to the U.S. Those were the heady days of the nationalist movement, in which we embraced secular, democratic values. However, Indira Gandhi, unlike her father, embraced a narrow commitment to personalistic power by fueling religious polarization. After her assassination, her associates within the Congress party channeled public grief into hatred of the Sikhs.

A small source of solace is that most citizens were appalled by the Congress party's actions. By early November, social workers, scholars, journalists, and other Delhi citizens came together to help the victims and their families. One of the first organizations to aid the survivors the Nagrik Ekta Manch, which worked in relief camps, provided documentation of the brutalities and helped unite divided families. The Manch became the focal point for volunteer relief and Amrita, Mark, and I joined in its efforts. The *gurdwaras* opened twenty relief camps and eventually the government created ten more. Nonetheless, the government's callous indifference to the victims is indescribable. The compensation it offered was demeaning: a paltry Rs. 10,000 ($357 at the 1985 exchange rate) to the next of kin if they could prove that their relative had died—which was often impossible, since they were burnt to death and only ashes remained. The government provided Rs. 2,000 ($71) for those who were considered seriously injured and Rs. 5,000 ($179) for a house or apartment that had been destroyed. These meager amounts spoke volumes as to how little value the government placed on Sikh lives and property.

Our family had earlier created Kabliji Trust, a philanthropic NGO. The organization designated two social workers to help families at a camp in Harinagar, near Delhi. I worked alongside these social workers in the tents they erected for displaced families. A large proportion of the survivors were women, perhaps because men were more apt to be recognizable as Sikhs because of their turbans and beards. The surviving women and children were traumatized. Many of them had witnessed their houses being burnt and destroyed, and their family members being tortured and killed. We distributed food, clothes, utensils, rations, and bedding to the survivors. What was much harder was addressing their deep psychological wounds. I was traumatized myself by the stories I heard and by the looted homes I visited. How could I offer sympathy and support to the widows and mothers who had experienced such unbelievable suffering? How could I possibly mitigate their pain or even explain it? I am still haunted by the image of a young widow with two sons. The younger one, who was eight years old, had been a mute witness to the horrors. He would leave the camp in the morning, collect matchboxes for sale and wander out. Sometimes he would return at night and sometimes disappear for a day or more, leaving his mother distraught. During the month that I worked at the camp, not one official from the central government or Delhi administration visited the camp. Only the Sikh Gurdwara Committee and its volunteers kept track of the victims' families and their needs.

Soon after the violence, a stream of international journalists visited Delhi. They called on my brother, Patwant, because of his connections with the media, and asked to visit the neighboring state of Haryana, where we had established a hospital—The Kabliji Hospital and Rural Health Care Center—with funds from our family trust. Our hospital compensated for the dearth of public hospitals in the area by providing eye care to the poor, predominantly Hindu community.

We learned that a group of angry Hindu men had gone to our hospital after Mrs. Gandhi's death, with the intention of murdering a Sikh doctor who resided there. Fortunately, news of the impending attack reached the hospital. The staff deftly evacuated the doctor by concealing him in a hospital gown on a stretcher and transporting him away in an ambulance. The mobs forced the hospital gates open and stormed through the premises. Unable to find any Sikhs, they left with their laden kerosene tins intact.

I drove with the journalists from the hospital to Patwant's nearby farm house. Although the exterior of the house was intact, the house had been badly ransacked. The beautiful Art Deco teak furniture, inherited from our parents, as well as carpets, paintings and other works of art were missing. As we entered his house, his cow and calf were being led on the Sona Road.

I took the journalists to the nearest police station, where I found our family furniture with people sprawled on the sofas and chairs, desks piled with dusty files and dirty tea cups. When I accused the police of having stolen the furniture, they replied matter of factly that they had taken it for safekeeping. Our belongings were never returned or seen again. The events that I witnessed taught me how religiously motivated violence can give rise to crass greed. Once authorities have turned a blind eye or, worse yet, become complicit in the violence, people step into the vacuum and steal. I was reminded of similar events during the Partition violence, when my parents had reprimanded our servants for stealing shoes and clothes from a Muslim shop that Hindu mobs had looted.

My own farm house, not far from Patwant's, was a wreck. It had been built while I was still in the States. It was a square stone house built in the traditional pattern of a haveli with a courtyard in the center, surrounded on all sides by verandahs, which were designed to provide shaded spaces from the strong summer sun and monsoon rains and keep the rooms cool. The house had beautiful solid wood doors and French windows that we had bought from auctions of old British-style houses which were being torn down to make room for modern buildings. The roof was made of terra cotta tiles and solid wood beams.

My farm house in Haryana

The doors and windows had been burnt and in some rooms the roof had collapsed. During my UN posting in Bangkok, I had stopped periodically in Delhi enroute to New York to supervise the construction and put finishing touches on the house. But I had not spent a single night in it. I was planning to spend time there while working at the family hospital upon my return to India. I had not even insured the house, thinking I would do so when I was back in Delhi. I could not afford to rebuild it on that scale or style, nor could I imagine making a home in a place where I had been made to feel so unwanted. I sat on a rock in front of the house and wept uncontrollably.

A few months later, Patwant and I decided to sell our farmhouses and close that chapter of our lives. A whole life and career ended with a strange twist. A house of my dreams, which I would never live in, had been destroyed. My plans for my future life were in shreds. More than ever, I wondered where my home was. My two sets of parents, who had always been my home, had passed away. My daughters were living in the States and were only likely to visit for short periods of time. Romen was still very uncertain as to where his home was and whether he wanted to live full time in Delhi. His preoccupation with writing poetry and fiction gave him an anchor, which I didn't have. My anchor had been my family, home, and country—all of which now seemed to be lost.

After I collected myself, I sought to come to terms with my grief and bewilderment by gaining a deeper understanding of the events that had unfolded. Why had the Congress party demonstrated such hostility towards the Sikhs? What basis was there to its allegation that Sikh separatists represented a national security threat and thus had to be brutally exterminated? In early 1985, I accompanied Madhu Kishwar, editor of the feminist journal *Manushi*, to Sangrur district in southern Punjab. Madhu had been active in Nagrik Ekta Manch and had written extensively about the Sikh carnage. We decided to meet with Harchand Singh Longowal (respectfully known as Sant Longowal) who had been the president of the Sikh party, the Akali Dal, during the Punjab insurgency of the 1980s. He struck me as a gentle, kind, thoughtful person. He spent hours speaking with us very openly. When we asked him how he explained the growth of the Sikh secessionist movement, he responded that the prime minister had bolstered the extremist faction of the Sikhs in order to undermine the Akali Dal party because its growing popularity presented a threat to Congress dominance. He provided us with extensive evidence and documentation of how this had happened. He insisted that the crisis in Punjab was political rather than religious. We pressed him on how his religious commitments influenced his views of gender relations and were pleasantly surprised to learn that he strongly supported full property and inheritance rights for women. After our meeting, Sant Longowal went on to sign a peace accord with Rajiv Gandhi that reduced tensions in Punjab; tragically, Longowal was assassinated shortly thereafter. My meeting with him left an indelible impression and drew me back to Sangrur years later, this time to address agrarian indebtedness. But that is the subject of a later chapter.

eight

MY DELHI HOME AND WORK

One of the most rewarding aspects of my return to India was the opportunity to work with women on women's issues. Although I had spent my formative childhood years in India and had personally experienced sexism, all my professional work on women's rights until this point had been on global issues. I was eager to interact with Indian feminists and contribute to their work. I was fortunate to know some remarkable feminists, including Lotika Mitra, Vina Mazumdar, the director of the Center for Women's Development Studies (CWDS), Ila Bhatt, the founder of the Self-Employed Women's Association (SEWA), and Devaki Jain, co-founder of Development Alternatives for Women for a New Era (DAWN). I became friends with many other feminists, including Ritu Menon and Urvashi Butalia, who had established the first feminist publishing house, Kali for Women. After working with Devaki in DAWN, I decided to form a women's NGO myself.

In 1988, I created Ekatra, which means unity or togetherness in Hindi. I assembled a small, dedicated team, including Rekha Bezbarouah, Jayanti Banerjee, and Tara Appachu. We later hired several additional staff members, including Ghazala Khan. We appointed a board of directors and set up an office in rooms of my home. We worked hard in the mornings, would break for lunch in the garden where Romen often joined us, and returned to work in the afternoon.

With Ghazala Khan in Delhi

Ekatra's major goal was to work in partnership with other NGOs on research and advocacy about and for women. Our team had the skills and experience to do research and documentation, evaluate existing programs, train field workers, and write up reports. We wanted to understand the economic, social and political causes of Indian women's oppression by exploring obstacles to their access to land, employment, political representation, as well as the impact on women of parental son preference, the dowry system and religious persecution.

Our first step was to determine what kinds of research and policy initiatives the government and NGOs had undertaken so that we could determine what gaps we could fill and contributions we could make. We contacted a number of NGOs to explore possibilities for collaboration. We worked at different times with CWDS, SEWA, Peoples Rural Education Movement (PREM), and the International Center for Ethnic Studies in Colombo. We then got busy writing grant proposals. We received grants from Swedish, Canadian and particularly Norwegian development foundations.

Orissa Odyssey with Forest and Coastal Women

In 1990, the Norwegian Aid Program (NORAD) commissioned us to do an evaluation of the NGO PREM, which worked with women in coastal and forest areas of Orissa. Two Catholic priests who founded PREM had dedicated themselves to literacy training and other programs designed to improve women's conditions. A few years after establishing PREM, the brothers had to return to responsibilities in the Church. However, they had assembled a dedicated team of young women who lived and worked in the villages. We met with them and hired a social worker fluent in Oriya and tribal dialects.

I always had a very special place in my heart for Orissa, with its abundance of beautiful temples and erotic sculpture, crafts, forests, coastline, countryside, as well as its ethnically diverse people. So, when the opportunity to visit Orissa presented itself, I rushed to avail of it.

My colleague Rekha, some members of PREM, our assistant and I, took a jeep to visit one of the PREM centers. We drove through luscious green and wooded areas, along hilly and winding roads with innumerable species of birds and animals including wild cats. We arrived at a remote village. There in a bare room seated on mats were some twenty to thirty women of varying ages, accompanied by babies and children. They were tribal women who lived in the forests and had walked for two and a half hours on foot paths through the fields and mountains to see us. They were tall, statuesque and had ebony black skin. Their comportment was dignified. The older women had deep furrowed tattoo marks on their cheeks and foreheads. I had never seen Indian women who had such markings and I was fascinated and mystified.

Through our interpreter, who translated my questions from Hindi into Oriya and then from Oriya to their tribal dialects, we were able to converse. After we had spoken for a while I ventured to ask why the older women had markings on their foreheads. Was it a form of identification or initiation? Why didn't the younger women bear these markings? They informed me that British forest officials had sexually harassed and raped them. To "protect" them, the male elders had disfigured their faces so they would be less attractive. The younger tribal women were spared those marks.

They narrated their sad stories in flat, affectless tone. They had always lived in the forests, which they relied on for food, fuel and fodder for their animals. However, their peaceful lives and means of livelihood were disrupted when truckloads of men arrived and started summarily chopping down the forest trees. When they objected, these men responded that the government had authorized the felling of trees for commercial purposes. Besides, these tribals could not live in the forests unless they had land titles, which they lacked. This land had always been communally owned, they told us. Their ancestors, as far back as they knew, had been born, lived and died here and their spirits now resided here. They had lived in harmony with the flora and fauna of the forests. Suddenly they were being uprooted and their entire way of life was threatened. Forest contractors would destroy their homes and fine them if they gathered forest produce. I was struck by the cruelty of laws that claimed to protect the environment and sometimes even protected animals but cared little for forest dwelling tribals. We met with forest officials and told them that we found their practices cruel and inhumane. Alas, I fear our words had little impact.

We also learned from PREM members about the plight of the fisherwomen and their families who worked and lived on the coast. They had always made their livelihood from catching and selling fish and shrimps. However, mechanized trawlers in Orissa, as in other parts of India, were depleting locally consumed fish. Urbanization, tourism and industrial development were driving up the costs of coastal land. Like forest dwelling tribals, these fishing communities rarely had legal titles to their coastal homes and were forced to move inland. They told us that they had settled a few miles from the coast but were displaced once again because a highway was being constructed where they lived. They now had to commute long distances to their place of work.

We provided NORAD with a very positive account of the work that PREM was doing and encouraged it to fund additional housing for members of the fishing community who had been displaced from their land.

Temple Prostitutes

Ekatra secured NORAD funding to work on another project, on temple prostitutes in Andhra Pradesh. Among the temple prostitutes were Venkatesan and the slightly better off Joginis who were members of the Dommara community. (Elsewhere they were known as Devadasis or Basivis.)

The system of temple prostitution had existed for decades but whereas in the past these women were trained in classical music and dance and lived in their patrons' homes, their conditions had steadily deteriorated. Low caste, poverty-stricken families turned their daughters over to temple prostitution as a source of income. Most of these families either owned small plots of land or were landless wage laborers. They experienced chronic droughts and their livelihoods were precarious. Thus, they resorted to marrying their teenage daughters to the Goddess Yellama in a ceremony that Hindu priests performed. They would put a symbolic *tikka* on the girls' heads and a bracelet around their wrists. The priests would take the girls to live in the temple. When the girls reached puberty, the priests would sexually "initiate" them and then auction them off to the highest bidders.

It was very difficult to get to meet these temple prostitutes but we found an opening. We learned of a young Venkatasani who had married a policeman, left the business and moved to another town. She had become a strong opponent of the practice; she spoke with us at length and introduced us to a number of women in the trade.

We tried to convince the temple prostitutes we met to leave their trade and learn other skills from which they could earn an income. Not surprisingly, we were unsuccessful. The women told us that they made more money in this business than they otherwise would and neither had the time nor inclination to learn new skills. The Joginis were especially resistant to change. They were generally sold to village chiefs or affluent farmers who bought them houses in exchange for their services. These women had their children as well as their parents and siblings live with them. The Joginis' parents did not object to their daughters' work since they were beneficiaries.

Interestingly, we found that the Venkatasanis and Joginis demonstrated preference for their daughters and would provide them with better nourishment than their sons, since they expected their girls to follow them in the trade and support their mothers in old age. Many of the neglected young boys became involved in petty crime. We encouraged the Venkatasanis to send their children to school. A few of them agreed to let their sons attend boarding schools and daughters attend day schools. We also recommended that NORAD create scholarships for children to attend school.

We organized a few health camps. Fortunately, the AIDS epidemic had not spread to this group but some were treated for venereal diseases. They were also provided with contraceptives and taught how to treat minor illnesses. We repeated the camps after six months for further check-ups and arranged counselling and preventive care.

We came away from these experiences with a heightened awareness of how little the government was doing to address the needs of its most vulnerable and exploited citizens. We could see from our conversations with forest officials that they did not have the slightest interest in what we had to say, in part because they were pilfering profits. As laudable as the work of some NGOs was, many resources went towards organizational maintenance and little was left for the recipients. My experiences on the ground made me aware of a far more distressing reality than I had imagined.

Female Feticide and Dowry

Ekatra decided to focus on female feticide and dowry-related violence in 2004. Our first step was to do surveys in Haryana, Himachal Pradesh and Punjab. After filing our reports, we wanted to find another medium through which to raise consciousness about these practices. We decided to make films on these issues and commissioned Anwar Jamal, a film maker, to direct them. One of the films, *The Third Way*, was a docu-drama about a courageous young woman who refused to submit to pressures by her husband and in-laws to abort her female fetus. The other, *Vanishing Daughters*, was on dowry related violence. Both films identified the possibilities for women's resistance to patriarchal practices. These experiences laid the ground work for my work among destitute farmers in Punjab.

nine

AMIDST KALISHNIKOVS AND ROCKET ATTACKS IN AFGHANISTAN

The United Nations Development Program (UNDP) invited me to serve as senior special advisor on integrating women into the planning process in Afghanistan. Soumendu Banerjee, the United Nations Resident Representative, welcomed me warmly and provided me with an office, clerical staff, and an assistant and interpreter named Sharifa. He gave me a map of the city, which indicated where it would be unsafe for me to visit. I did not always comply with this injunction—and learned a lot about Afghanistan as a result. The period of my assignment, 1986-1988, was an important and turbulent time in Afghanistan's history.

Romen and I had visited Afghanistan in the 1950s. We were taken by the country's rugged and harsh beauty, its people and its history, which was linked to ours. A notable Afghan leader, Muhammad Ghor, invaded India in 1175 and conquered a large territory. Subsequently the Lodhis, the Tughlaqs, and the Mughals came from Central Asia through Afghanistan and set up dynasties until the advent of British rule in the 19th century. I had vivid memories of Mazar-i-Sharif, the fourth largest city in Afghanistan and the capital of Balkh province, an important commercial center. In the city square was the mausoleum of Hazrat Ali, the prophet's son-in-law, that had been rebuilt in the 15th century after its destruction by Genghis Khan 200 years earlier.

Its strategic location, surrounded by the Soviet Union, China, Pakistan, and Iran, made Afghanistan a cross-roads and battleground between big and small powers. Never a cohesive nation with a centrally planned state, Afghanistan was always a series of large village settlements, linked together with narrow mountain passes that were snowbound in winter. It was a tribal society that was governed by strong kinship ties. Many nomadic tribes still followed the traditional routes which lead into both Iran and Pakistan. The Mujahideen controlled trade relations and smuggled goods across the border to Pakistan. Although the official exchange rate was $1 (U.S. currency) to 55 Afghanis, people who wielded influence were able to exchange money for almost four times that amount on the black market. Interestingly this black market was not underground at all. Moneylenders freely exchanged money out in the open. The money market was always bustling with people buying, selling, and exchanging different currencies with much bargaining and haggling.

Although the political landscape had changed since we were last there, the old landmarks survived. Kabul was always a traders' paradise and I loved wandering through the bazaars. We visited the money market, carpet shops, Tota bazaar, and Adams bazaar. Tota (meaning a piece of fabric) bazaar advertised "peace goods" by which it meant "piece goods" or fabric by the piece. On one side of the lane were shops with fabrics spread on chariots selling mostly Japanese fabrics but also some from the U.S., France, Italy, and Britain at prices cheaper than in the country of origin. We found tribal jewelry in silver and gold, inlaid with semi-precious stones and an abundance of pottery, brass ware, and ceramics old and new, real and fake. Genuine Rosenthal and Limoge porcelains interspersed chipped, cheap reproductions. The carpet shops were second in economic importance to this huge bovine-based economy. Shar-i-Nau was the retail carpet center.

The retail trade was almost entirely in the hands of Tajiks, Pashtuns or Hazaras. Chaman Khuzuri had a long line of two-story

buildings where exporters, middlemen, brokers and carpet deal-
ers and their warehouses and shops were located. Upstairs, the
rooms were occupied by Turkmans and Uzbeks visiting Kabul
from the north to conduct business. Along with these old markets
were signs of Soviet and Western influence. New shops selling
Russian goods had cropped up. Not only could one buy micro-
wave ovens, refrigerators, air conditioners, and electronic goods
but also the best vodka and caviar.

Gender inequality was stark in Afghanistan. A good indication was the sex ratio. According to the 1979 census, there were
7.83 million women as against 8.31 million men. Women's comportment was considered a mark of men's honor and women
were punished for defying social norms. The custom of *badal* or
exchange prevailed. A girl or women, however young or old, sister
or daughter, could be given away to resolve a conflict at the loss of
a duel or upon a *jirgah* or assembly's decision. Any male member
of the family, father, brother or son, could kill a woman if she was
seen talking to a man.

And yet I was deeply impressed by the many strong feminists
I encountered in Afghanistan. I met with the socialist feminist
leader, Anahita Ratebzad, who served as Afghanistan's deputy head of state from 1980-86 and founded the Democratic
Organization of Afghan Women (DOWA). She was an elegant,
charismatic woman who was outspoken in her support for gender equality. She told me that she was proud to have organized
the first international women's day gathering in Kabul and had
attended international conferences to promote women's rights.
She was eventually forced by the Mujahideen to leave and fled to
India in 1992.

Then there was the remarkable Meena Keshwar Kamal, who
founded the Revolutionary Association of Women of Afghanistan (RAWA) in 1977. RAWA organized underground schools
and health facilities for women and provided counselling for survivors of sexual violence. Continually threatened for engaging

in anti-jihadi activities, Meena was assassinated in her home in Quetta in 1987.

I was also impressed by the many "ordinary" women I met. Sharifa introduced me to some of them over tea at her home. The stories they told have stayed with me. Sharifa, who was 34 years old and single, had travelled to the US and earned her MA in Sociology at the University of Chicago. She was well read and conversant with feminist literature. This freedom was hard won. She lived at home, one of four sisters and seven brothers. Her father, a *mullah* (religious cleric) from the Pashtun tribe, harshly dominated his wife and daughters. Sharifa told me that she had become so depressed by her father's strictures that she tried to commit suicide by taking an overdose of sleeping pills when she was thirteen years old. What had finally pushed her over the edge was that she and her sister had dressed up for a wedding in rather flashy Indian clothes. Her father was infuriated and ordered them to change. Sharifa refused and did not attend the wedding. This followed a series of other incidents. Her brothers expected her to wait on them and to make them tea when they returned from school. They were accorded freedoms that were denied to her. The pressures and demands on her seemed endless. When her family saw how desperate she had become, they relented and allowed her to study abroad.

Sharifa introduced me to Nikob, a 27-year old woman who was studying reconstructive surgery. Medical schools in Kabul before the Saur revolution were among the best in the world. However, few women became doctors and those who did became obstetricians and gynecologists. Nikob opted instead to specialize in military surgery so that she could attend to the thousands of people who had suffered physical deformities, such as loss of limbs, amidst the civil war. Women surgeons were needed because most women patients did not want to see male doctors. Nikob says she was very fortunate to be working with unsexist male colleagues. Besides her government job, Nikob had a sizeable private practice and taught medical students at the Jamhuriat Hospital in Kabul. She said that unlike Sharifa, her father was very egalitarian in his views of women and in his relationship to her and her mother.

Twenty-seven-year old Malalai had graduated from medical school in 1985 and worked in a polyclinic as a radiotherapist. She took up medicine because she felt she could help the people most in need. She worked closely with cancer patients. She and her colleagues mixed freely during work but could not socialize after hours. The year she graduated, a majority of students in the program were women. She had received a scholarship and her education, board and lodging were free. Her family had supported her decision to study medicine. Her sister and Sharifa were her role models. She had learned from them that women should not be restricted by their gender from pursuing their ambitions. They should have choices and opportunities equal to men's. Why couldn't a woman be president, she asked?

Sima, who was 29, had an MA in engineering and worked in the Department of Construction of Highways. When she first started working there, there were 25 women out of a total of 1,500 employees. By 1987, the number of women doubled because men were involved in military service. Although she did not have any trepidation about choosing this male-dominated field, her male colleagues and professors clearly felt uncomfortable in her presence. The seat next to her was always empty at meetings and on staff buses. She said that conversations among her male colleagues became stiff and formal when she entered the room. Sima was troubled by the absence of women in the trade union. One day she organized a meeting that 125 women attended. They elected one woman from every department to represent them and elected Sima as chair. She worked there for four years. However, the management resented her activism and one day she found a letter on her desk informing her that she was being transferred.

All of these women yearned for freedom and sought to achieve it through education and professional employment. For Nikob and Malalai, medical practice provided an opportunity to make a social contribution while gaining the skills and income to achieve independence. Weaving these few stories into my overall impressions of government policies, I found that women were increasingly rebelling against the constraints on their freedom and finding multiple paths to enact change.

I arrived in Kabul in the spring of 1986, seven years after the Soviet Union had occupied Afghanistan. Soviet occupation of the cities was tenuous and it was limited to only about 20 percent of the countryside. The cities, including Kabul, were encircled by the Mujahideen, which comprised hundreds of guerilla groups who were internally divided but unified in their opposition to Soviet occupation.

Although I was a critic of Cold War rivalries that crushed aspirations for non-alignment in formerly colonized countries, I was impressed by the government's formal commitments to women's rights. I was also aghast by the U.S.-supported Mujahideen's attacks on women. The two years I spent in Afghanistan, from 1986-1988, marked a turning point in the escalation of violence against women.

The Soviet-led Democratic Republic of Afghanistan provided legal and constitutional guarantees of gender equality and non-discrimination on grounds of sex in education, employment and under civil law. The communist government created opportunities for women in education, employment, and adult literacy. It created day care centers and provided maternity benefits. This was born of both conviction and necessity, as men over the age of 18 were drawn into military service and many of them were killed or disabled. The government-supported Central Women's Club set up literacy courses and income generating projects for women. It integrated primary health care into mother and child health programs. It established three-month training programs for midwives. Although it did not have a family planning policy, it encouraged families to space their children by two or three years.

The average family size was between six and seven children.

The government gave me free access to bureaucrats and politicians, including the top-ranking policy makers and ministers. I had extensive meetings with officials and members of the WDOAW, the Central Women's Club, and the DYOA. I visited their literary classes, vocational training centers and crèches, and attended political rallies. I visited small-scale industries including raisin and nut processing plants, bakeries, tailoring factories and beauty parlors, a computer center and several cooperative enterprises. I met with women working in government offices, radio, television, journalism, and cinema.

I saw great advances in women's education and employment. Women were visible in the public sphere, many of them unveiled. During the Soviet occupation, female illiteracy declined from 98% to 75%. Women were employed in a range of fields, from factories to teaching, medicine, architecture, construction, and government service. Carpet weaving in Afghanistan was done exclusively by women on horizontal looms, unlike in Iran and India. In rural areas, however, there were fewer opportunities for women. They assisted men in agricultural activities but were not farmers themselves.

This is not to say that there was complete gender equality. Unjust patriarchal relations still prevailed in the workplace and in the family, with women occupying lower level sex-typed jobs. Although in principle the government was committed to involving women in development activities, its practice fell short. Legal and policy changes could not change deep seated prejudices towards women. Despite the progress women made in Kabul and in some other cities, traditional customs and attitudes remained unchanged in most of the country, especially within the home.

I wrote an exhaustive report for the UNDP on my assessment and recommendations. I emphasized the importance of bringing women into every aspect of development, and recommended increased budgetary allocations for programs designed to empower women, as well as the creation of a permanent secretariat on women and development in the State Planning Committee. I also recommended a number of steps which the western world, especially the U.S., could take to protect women's rights. I suggested that aid packages be contingent on the integration of women in development projects. I recommended that international women's colleges, vocational institutes, and NGOs provide fellowships to women to study abroad. Alas, the changing political climate rendered many of my proposals ineffective.

My final year in Kabul was very tense. April 26, 1988, was the tenth anniversary of the revolution. Tanks and military vehicles rolled down the streets. Fighter planes roared overhead, causing glass windows in houses to shatter. Trouble was expected and we were asked to stay indoors. However, the day passed peacefully, without incident.

However, on May 1st there was a loud explosion at 10:30 pm. My house shook as if it would collapse. It was a terrifying experience. The next day the Security Officer and three UN Military Advisors arrived at my house, surveyed the area and concluded that the damage had been caused by a powerful rocket, launched from a tank on the surrounding mountains, aimed at the nearby radio station. The Mujahideen launched attacks on the area where I lived over the next few days, killing a number of women and children. On TV, I saw the charred remains of a family in my neighborhood. Mujahideen violence was even more severe in the areas that they controlled outside the city.

I went to work as usual on May 14th, the day before the Soviet Union was scheduled to begin withdrawing its troops. My neighbors were busy stocking up on food supplies. Both urban but especially rural areas were suffering from a severe water shortage. Women had to carry water over long distances, store it and use it expeditiously. There was a high incidence of water-borne diseases.

On my way to the office, I saw posters on the walls warning residents, especially women, to remain in their houses. *Shabanamas* or handbills warned of reprisals against women found outside their homes. Followers of Gulbuddin Hekmatyar had started throwing acid on women who ventured out in western clothes which exposed their arms and legs. Ironically, the United States favored the so-called "freedom fighters" headed by Hekmatyar over more moderate Mujahideen groups. Saudi Arabian and American arms and ammunition gave the fundamentalists a vital edge over the moderates. Tragically, this military hardware was used to target unarmed civilians, most of them women and children.

In the years after my departure from Afghanistan, women were caught in the cross-fire of a brutal civil war. Since the Najibullah regime was anxious to accommodate the opposition under its National Reconciliation Policy, women's rights were made the first offering. The events that followed were worse than the direst predictions. The overthrow of the Najibullah government in 1992 led to fighting among warring fundamentalist groups. Massive artillery attacks killed and wounded thousands of civilians, especially women and children. Afghan women's rights were violated with impunity once Mujahideen groups seized power in Kabul. The ruling warlords dismantled the legal system and either assumed judicial functions themselves or accorded it to the Islamic clergy or local *shuras* (councils of elders). Trials were arbitrary and punishments were barbaric, like stoning to death and public lashings.

Rape by armed guards of the various warring factions was condoned by their leaders; it was viewed as a way of intimidating vanquished populations and of rewarding soldiers. Fear of rape drove women to suicide and fathers to kill their daughters so that other men would not "degrade" them. Scores of women were abducted and detained, sexually abused, and sold into prostitution. Innumerable girls were victimized and tortured. In addition to physical abuse, women were stripped of their fundamental rights of association, freedom of speech, employment, and movement.

With the formation of the Islamic state of Afghanistan in 1992, and particularly the appointment of Gulbuddin Hekmatyar as prime minister, matters got even worse. The Ministry of Islamic Affairs dismissed women from a number of different posts. It abolished co-education, which existed until this point to the sixth grade. The Supreme Court of the Islamic State issued an ordinance which decreed that women should wear a veil to cover the whole body and forbade them from leaving their homes.

If the period of Taliban rule represented a low point for women, the US war on Afghanistan, launched to avenge the attacks on the World Trade Center and Pentagon in 2001, simply contributed to continued upheaval. The Bush administration's claim that the downfall of the Taliban would bring about the liberation of women proved to be hollow. I knew enough of Afghanistan's history to realize how long, slow and hard the struggle for women's emancipation would be. And I was grateful to have been there during a period of fragile peace to witness the strength and determination of some remarkable Afghan women.

ten

WITNESSING LIFE IN THE CHAMBAL RAVINES

An unexpected adventure came my way in February 1996 when Mary Ann Weaver, a correspondent for The New Yorker magazine, asked if I would travel with her to the Chambal ravines, a region in Madhya Pradesh, adjoining Uttar Pradesh and Rajasthan She had been commissioned to do a story on Phoolan Devi, the notorious bandit queen, and needed an interpreter for the interviews. I took five days off from my work for Ekatra to travel first for five hours by train to Gwalior and then for three hours to the ravines and the forests.

Phoolan Devi had been in the news for some time. She was the subject of the Bollywood film, *The Bandit Queen*, which she later sued for mis-representing her, and the subject of a biography. Phoolan Devi's story was mesmerizing. A poor low caste woman, her parents had married her to an abusive man when she was just a teenager. She escaped and joined a gang of bandits, one of whom became her lover. She was the only female member of the gang and she was often brutally beaten and raped. She proved to be as powerful as any man in the gang and in 1983 was imprisoned for eleven years for participating in a massacre of upper caste men who had killed her lover. The tide had turned with the growth of lower caste politics and Phoolan Devi had achieved increasing notoriety. The Chief Minister of Uttar Pradesh, Mulayam Singh

Yadav, also a member of a lower caste, released her and dismissed all charges against her in 1994. Phoolan Devi launched a political career by planning to run for Parliament.

Mary Anne not only wanted to interview Phoolan Devi, which she had earlier done on another trip, but also to meet with the men Phoolan Devi had worked with. She also wanted to acquire an in-depth understanding of the bandit system. According to Malkan Singh, a former dacoit, the *baaghi* (rebel) system as the dacoits described it, dated back to the eleventh century when the Chauhan Kings ruled Delhi. Legend has it that Prithvi Raj, one of the king's nephews, usurped the throne in his absence and the king took to the ravines in Madhya Pradesh. The *baaghis* trace their ancestry to him.

The *baaghis* established an alternate form of government, complete with their own army, police, chiefs and deputy chiefs. Their code of conduct was rigid and strictly enforced. The chief had to approve all major decisions regarding who was to be killed or kidnapped, what ransom would be demanded, and how funding for guns and other ammunition would be secured. The chief did not even share this information with the deputy for the simple reason that should the deputy turn informant both he and the whole gang could be decimated.

On a crisp fall morning, Mary Anne, Bob Nickelsberg, a photographer from Time magazine, and I met at the Delhi railway station to catch the Shatabdi Express to Gwalior. It was a good time of the year to be travelling. Yellow mustard fields interspersed with arid countryside lined both sides of the railroad track. About half way through our trip, the landscape became starker. There was a hint of the ravines in the distance.

Gwalior was all decked up with marigold flowers and colorful banners to welcome its favorite son, Maharaja Madhavrao Scindia, a minister in the Narasimha Rao government. Gwalior was hosting one of the world series cricket matches and Scindia, a great cricket enthusiast, was attending. Although he had been accused of having taken money in a scam, his constituents in Gwalior totally rejected the charge and had prepared a hero's welcome. Their rationale was that, since he was already so wealthy, why would he take more by illegal means? Madhavrao was no bandit in their eyes.

We arrived at the Usha Kiran Palace Hotel- a palace with arches and domes built in the Rajasthani architectural style- set in a beautiful garden. At a press conference that evening for Madhavrao to which we were invited, he was most affable and hospitable. After his official press conference ended, the discussion centered around Phoolan Devi and the dacoits.

We were told that the dacoits had terrorized the Chambal region where the ravines and terrain were conducive to their activities. They had become a threat to motorists driving at night on the main highways as well as on the ancillary roads. In 1982, Jayaprakash Narayan, a respected political leader and disciple of the Gandhian principle of non-violence, declared an amnesty for all bandits who came forward and surrendered their arms. In return, the government would drop all charges against them, give them houses, small pensions and land to cultivate to facilitate their reintegration into society. Both government and *baaghi* representatives signed the agreement and an NGO, the Gandhi Peace Foundation, made arrangements for the surrender. The uncrowned bandit kings of the region, like Mohr Singh and Malkit Singh, along with several hundred lesser known dacoits surrendered, leaving only a hundred or so to remain outlaws.

Mary Anne arranged with the Police Department to have the retired Deputy Commander of Police, Raghunandan Sharma, accompany us to the ravines and arrange for us to meet with some of the top *baaghi* leaders. Mr. Sharma turned out to be a key player in the story.

The next morning, we set out in two cars. Bob went in one, which he filled with his photographic equipment. Mary Anne, Mr. Sharma, and I travelled in the other. Enroute, Mr. Sharma stopped at his house to show us various photographs and citations that he had received for capturing and killing a record number of dacoits. He sat in the back seat between Mary Anne and me, with a loaded gun on his lap. He claimed that he was carrying it for our protection, as there were still over a hundred dacoits at large in the ravines and in the forests. He spent most of the two hours regaling us with stories of his brave encounters with the dacoits. When he wasn't talking, he was napping—which was hair raising, since his loaded gun swayed to and fro between Mary Anne's knees and mine. We feared that it would go off at any minute.

A short distance from the ravines we stopped and looked down at a beautiful, winding river that was surrounded by flowers. But the river was filled with the fiercest looking crocodiles I have ever seen. I found the site so terrifying that I had to look away.

We passed a temple dedicated to the Hindu Goddess Durga that the dacoits had built at the top of the mountain. The *baaghis* are very religious, god fearing people, and worshippers of the Goddess Durga, who has the power to destroy evil. They usually visited the Durga temple and made offerings to the goddess before and after engaging in killings and kidnappings. However, if pressed for time, they would honk their horns as a salutation and promise to visit and pay their respects in person later.

After crossing the bridge on the Chambal river, we saw the ravines. Dry with hard caked earth, they were breathtakingly harsh. How long had those earth formations been there? Even goats had a hard time navigating the deep ravines. How could humans survive in those brutal canyons without water, food or shelter, all of which had to be transported from outside? We tried to walk down but found it impossible to do so. Only Bob managed to descend a short distance to take some pictures for the story.

A half hour's drive took us to the village of Jora where we were scheduled to meet Mohr Singh, a top dacoit gang leader, and his most trusted lieutenant and second in the gang's command, Ram Charan Singh. We were taken to the *dak bungalow* (guest house), where Ram Charan and Mohr Singh met us. Mohr Singh, at 62 and over six feet tall, had a commanding personality, a wrestler's build, waxed moustaches and stern demeanor. He had a red *tikka* (ritual mark) on his forehead. He was elegantly dressed in a flowing white *kurta-pajama* (tunic and pants) and vest with a long silk scarf and a big gun slung by a strap from his shoulder. He was flanked by Ram Charan Singh on one side, also armed with a gun that was as tall as him, and his lawyer on the other side. It was an impressive array of men who looked like courtiers or religious priests from a princely state, not that different from the figure of Madhavrao Scindia.

After we were introduced, Mohr Singh looked somewhat disdainfully at Mary Anne and me. How was it women's business to discuss dacoity, I imagine he must have been thinking. However, overcoming his initial trepidation, he offered us tea and settled into a friendly conversation. The interview began with Mary Anne asking questions in English and my translating them into Hindi. How many men had Mohr Singh killed and what other crimes had he committed? How much money did he have? How had he adjusted to his present life as a law-abiding citizen? What did he think of Phoolan Devi? As I tried to interpret the questions and answers it turned out that each person in the room was trying to show his mastery of the English language. Mary Anne who was blessed with a more resonant voice than me, repeatedly had to bring the meeting under control.

Mohr Singh acknowledged that he had killed over 400 people and kidnapped many more for ransom, to say nothing of other heinous crimes listed under the Indian Penal Code. He recounted that he had 125 men in his gang and they patrolled 180 miles of the ravines. He had 3,500,000 Indian Rupees, the equivalent of US $100,000 at the time, when he was captured. But he had not saved any of it. The *baaghis* had to spend far more money on their daily needs than most people. The shopkeepers charged them inflated rates to compensate for the risks entailed in selling goods to dacoits. The dacoits also provided patronage to the villagers, paying for their daughters' marriages, dowries, feasts and funeral expenses.

Mohr Singh objected to being described as a bandit. He said that he was a *baaghi*, a rebel. His most important goal was to regain land which he believed belonged to his family. He would fight, kill and die for land. The sins of fathers were visited upon their sons. Their deaths were avenged by their children. The arm of the law was distant and slow. So, bandits took matters in their own hands for rough and ready justice. Banditry, he stressed, was a preferable system of justice to that of the government with all its "scams" that were well publicized by the press.

Mohr Singh was happy to lay down his arms and lead a normal life with his family when the Indian government declared an amnesty for the dacoits. He was elected as head of the Council of Malegoan and enjoyed a good reputation. He received a small farm and house as part of the amnesty. He lived there with his 42-year old wife, who was a school teacher, and their two children.

Mary Anne asked Mohr Singh his views of Phoolan Devi. He scowled and said, condescendingly, that he did not think much of her. She hadn't killed a single person in a police encounter but had cold bloodedly massacred innocent people point blank. This was not true bravery. In any case, the ravines were no place for women, he said. They had proved to be the downfall of the *baaghis* as they became informants under pressure. Mohr Singh was ready to be a protector to women but was unwilling to see them as equals. Before parting he promised to be a brother to Mary Anne and me. If we ever needed help we could call on him.

As the evening was descending. Mr. Sharma informed us that if we wanted to visit the forest we should do it fast as it was still full of dacoits. The forest was beautiful with rolling hills and luscious vegetation along the banks of a tributary of the Chambal river, that had been dammed for hydro-electric power. The glorious setting sun reflected in the water gave it a magical quality of peace and tranquility. We passed by the outskirts of the forest, but it was too dangerous to enter in the dark. We drove three hours to Gwalior sitting on either side of Mr. Sharma and his loaded gun. The gun seemed more menacing than the dacoits.

Our remaining goals were to visit the maximum-security Gwalior jail and find a way of meeting the elusive Malkan Singh, another top dacoit leader. Although Mary Anne had planned to meet the superintendent of the jail, neither he nor his deputy were available. The good news, our driver informed us, was that that we could visit Malkan Singh at his home. He drove us through narrow lanes and alleys and took us to Malkan Singh's house. We were met by Malkan Singh and his brother. He presented a strong contrast to Mohr Singh. Although he had the reputation of being a formidable dacoit, he looked unassuming. He had a small build, was dressed simply, was unarmed and didn't have a *tikka* on his forehead.

Malkan Singh was hostile from start to finish. We subsequently understood why: the police had shot and killed his 21-year old nephew despite the fact that the government had declared an amnesty. His nephew's widow and child were living with him. Malkan's tirade was along the following lines: the government was corrupt; politicians made false promises; the police were ruthless and engaged in random violence and journalists made money from writing about it. None of them cared in the least for justice. Malkan, like Mohr, stressed that they were *baaghis* and not bandits and they tried to solve land disputes which the government refused to address. They believed in robbing the rich and paying the poor.

Setting aside moral judgments about the use of violence, the story of the bandits is an impressive account of human endurance against odds of nature and man. It is a story of discipline and defiance with underpinnings of religious beliefs and a rough and ready system of justice born out of disillusionment. It is clearly a man's world, informed by a code of conduct where women are unwelcome. And yet Phoolan Devi had managed to hold her own and become a heroine for the poor and dispossessed. I came away from the ravines deeply impressed by her powers of endurance.

Haunted by these powerful images and insights, we had to make a rapid transition into a different world: from a taxi to the train, to the New Delhi railway station, to the comforts of home at 11, Amrita Sher-Gil Marg.

Front of the house at Amrita Sher-Gil Marg

eleven

RETURN TO PUNJAB

Romen and I settled into our Delhi home, while spending long summers with our children, sons-in-law and grandchildren. Romen started a book publishing company that translated works from regional languages into English and also published several books of his own. We divided the summer months into three parts: New York, where we caught up with old friends; Amherst, where we visited Amrita, Mark and their kids; and Des Moines, where we visited Rekha and her family. Romen added to this a month or two in Europe. He stayed in the small apartment overlooking Lake Trevignano outside of Rome where Rekha and Rob had gone on their honeymoon, as well as an apartment that he purchased in Paris.

One of our sons in law, Rob, was Italian-American; the other, Mark, was a Francophile, so Romen bought these places with them in mind. We would laugh at how Romen, who spoke with a Bengali accent that had eluded even a touch of an American accent, could go native wherever he was. While in Paris, he would settle down at a neighborhood café, beret in hand, a glass of pastis by his side, and contemplate the passing scene. Every place he visited would inspire a story or a poem.

However, Romen's health was declining and travel was becoming more difficult. It was hard to come to terms with the increasing frailty of a man of boundless energy who had had always exuded such a passion for life. But Romen accepted restrictions on his mobility and found pleasure in his immediate surroundings. He especially marveled at the beauties of nature. He would sit in our garden at Amrita Sher-Gil Marg in the early morning hours, busily writing, look up with a smile and ask whether I'd like to hear his morning's "five-minute poem" over breakfast. We became extremely close in his final years. I took very good care of him and he appreciated my attention. My companion of sixty years passed away on September 23, 2007.

With Romen at our 50th wedding anniversary

Meanwhile my Delhi family expanded after Patwant married Meher Wilshaw. After Romen's death, the three of us spent almost every evening together. Meher gradually took over responsibilities for running the Kabliji Hospital in Haryana and added a school to the premises. Patwant was becoming increasingly frail and passed away on August 8, 2009. Patwant was a commanding presence and the house felt empty without him.

Patwant, me and Meher

Presenting a kirpan (Sikh honorific sword) to Patwant

With Patwant

*With Meher in a sculpture installation by the artist Manav Gupta
in my garden at Amrita Sher-Gil Marg*

Just three women, Meher, Ghazala (who moved out of her rented apartment and moved in with me), and I lived in the large family home that had once, to paraphrase the title of one of Romen's books, been a house full of people. We sought to re-establish our old routines and became even more immersed in our work.

Rao, my cook, me, and Savitri, my housekeeper

Meher spent three days each week supervising the Kabliji Hospital and school. I continued to spend summer months with the family in the States and they visited me in Delhi each year. I was especially thrilled when my grandsons, Romen, Raj, Ishan, and Javed, visited me on their own. On one memorable visit, scenes from the film *The Reluctant Fundamentalist* were shot in our home and I was thrilled that Javed acted in it. The film was directed by our dear friend Mira Nair, and Shabana Azmi and Om Puri were in it.

My home transformed into a set for shooting scenes from the film
The Reluctant Fundamentalist by Mira Nair

With Javed

I've also been blessed by wonderful new family members: Raj's wife Aadhithi and her parents, who have become dear friends.

Aadhiti and Raj at their wedding

And Ishan's beautiful son, Elijah, is my great-grandson, so my homes in the world have continued to grow and expand.

Javed, Ishan, Elijah, and Romen

To backtrack a bit, the focus of my work shifted during this period. Having done research and advocacy in several different regions of India, I now wanted to devote my energies to the Punjab. I contemplated working on a variety of issues when an article in the *Tribune* newspaper (August 11, 2005) caught my eye. It described massive indebtedness that was driving farmers, mostly men, to commit suicide in rural Punjab. Consequently, aging grandparents were often responsible for caring for grandchildren children after their sons' death. The article identified a human rights activist, Inderjit Singh Jaijee, a former Member of the Legislative Assembly from Sangrur district and chair of the Movement Against State Repression (MASR), an NGO that he helped form in 1987 to document human rights abuses in Punjab. MASR

had been gathering statistics on farmers suicides in Punjab's Sangrur and Mansa districts since 1998 and advocating on behalf of
the state's farmers. The article quoted Jaijee as saying:

> In all, more than 10,000 farmers have committed sui-
> cide in Punjab. Most of these families are now being
> headed by women...Statistics show that an average
> of 50 suicides take place in Lehra and Andana blocks
> every year. Even if we were to halve this number to 25,
> we could expostulate the number to 2,500 per year in
> Punjab's remaining 100 districts since suicide reports
> are now coming from all regions.

I decided that I had to meet Jaijee. I had grown up thinking of
Punjab as the land of plenty. I could not reconcile what I had read
with the images I still held of robust, healthy farmers who had
made Punjab the breadbasket of India.

When I called Jaijee and introduced myself, he invited me to
come see the situation for myself. A few days later I boarded a
train to Sangrur. I was Jaijee's guest in his large, old sprawling
house that he had inherited from his family. Although he came
from a family of considerable means, he lived the simple life of a
committed political activist. His home was open to anyone who
wanted to stay and his kitchen, like a *langar* in a *gurdwara,* served
simple, delicious vegetarian meals. I would return to this home
many times in the years to come.

In addition to creating an activist organization, Jaijee had
opened a degree college and a vocational training institute for
disadvantaged rural youth, which provided 300 scholarships for
young women in families that had experienced a suicide.

I went with Jaijee to some of the worst affected villages, in
Lehra and Moonak subdivisions of Sangrur district. I learned
about the causes of farmers' distress. The so-called green revolution, followed by neo-liberal reforms, which emphasized capital

intensive, mono-crop, export-oriented production, had increased class stratification and placed increasing burdens on small land-owners. Chemical fertilizers and pesticides were costly and interest rates on loans were high. Under the pressure of escalating costs, declining soil fertility, dwindling yields and mounting debt, small and marginal farmers were killing themselves, leaving their spouses, children and ageing parents in utter penury. The suicide rate was alarmingly high and rising. According to Jaijee, Punjab suffered among the highest rates of farmers' suicide in the country: between 40,000 and 60,000 from 1990 to 2010—far higher than the official government figure of 2,000 suicides during this period.

If there was little public awareness about the fate of Punjabi farmers, even less was known of the hardships women faced. I learned that the farming community's patriarchal structure leaves women ill-equipped to cope with challenges and responsibilities that result from the loss of male breadwinners. Women are prohibited by social custom from ploughing and doing many other forms of agricultural work, so they must hire men to perform these tasks. Moneylenders harass them to repay their husbands' debts while charging exorbitant interest on the high debts their husbands had accrued. They often confiscate women's land and houses when women are unable to pay off their loans. Children are forced to drop out of school and must start working at young ages. Women do not receive social security and lack access to credit. Often the land on which they live is not even registered in their names.

Certain Punjabi family practices compound women's vulnerability. When a farmer dies, his widow is expected to marry his brother, regardless of her own wishes, and even if he is already married. This practice, despite its claims to protect women, was designed to keep the land in the male dominated family. As a result, a woman can be passed on as chattel or sexual objects.

I decided to produce a film documenting the impact of the

agrarian crisis on farmers, and particularly on their widows. Anwar Jamal, who had made two short documentaries for Ekatra, directed *Harvest of Grief*. I accompanied the film team when they began shooting in Sangrur in February 2009. I will never forget some of the stories we recorded on film.

We entered the dusty, village of Bhutal Khurd, and entered the decrepit house where Darshan Singh's widow lived with her two children, a 10-year-old girl and an 8-year-old boy. She told us that she had no idea how large her husband's debt was and what anguish he was experiencing in the last days of his life. I was struck by how men's sense of pride and the humiliation they experienced at failing to live up to social expectations led them to feel a sense of personal failure and shame and to keep secrets from their wives. She wished that her husband had confided in her. Such were the consequences for both women and men of prevailing social norms.

Each story we heard was more heart-breaking than the next: of Roop Singh who had committed suicide, leaving behind his widow and daughter, Gurmeet Kaur; 13-year-old Jasvir Kaur who along with her two brothers lived with her grandmother since her father Lal Singh committed suicide; Rani Kaur, whose husband, two brothers in laws and nephew all committed suicide; Rajni and Gurdial Kaur, sisters who lived together with their children after both their husbands had committed suicide.

We learned that the pain of family members' suicides was exacerbated by inadequate government compensation and the paltry opportunities for women to earn a livelihood. The only women who expressed hope were those who could imagine supporting themselves. Gurmeet Kaur was grateful to have received a scholarship to attend college and Najma Khan, another widow, was earning an income through tailoring.

Harvest of Grief tells the stories of these and other families. It devotes particular attention to the plight of mothers and grandmothers who must support their families, repay debts and educate their children. It provides an account of the multiple causes of the current crisis, describes the government's discriminatory policies towards Punjab, in part because of its predominantly Sikh population, and critiques the human costs of economic liberalisation. It includes interviews with agricultural scientists, members of farmers' unions, and government officials.

We raised funds for *Harvest of Grief* from foundations and some private donors. One of the most generous among them was my very dear friend Jean Beard who has been there for me at the most important times of my life.

With Jean Beard

Our first screenings were in Punjab, then in other parts of India and the US. The film became a catalyst for discussions of agrarian indebtedness and farmers' suicides in many different parts of the world. I remember how a woman from a farming community in

Des Moines who was in the audience at a film screening, spoke of her own husband's suicide because of the debts he had incurred to maintain the family farm.

Shortly after the film was released, the Punjab government adopted one of the film's recommendations—to provide land titles in women's names. But I realized that there were no NGOs working with women in Sangrur, government programs remained scant, and much work was needed to improve their condition. Spurred by this realization, in 2016 I created an NGO, Building Bridges India (BBI), under the aegis of the Kabliji Memorial Trust, New Delhi, which my brother Patwant had founded, to work with the widows of farmers who had committed suicide. We secured additional funding from foundations, including the Buddhist Global Relief, and other sources. Our mission statement read:

> Building Bridges India represents a bridge from the past to the future; from a patriarchal society to an egalitarian one in which women have role options, rights and responsibilities; a passage from despair to hope.

We began by addressing women's health. Poor nutrition and ill health are endemic in rural India but are especially acute for female household heads. BBI did blood and urine tests on 150 women which showed that they suffered from moderate to severe anemia, hook warm parasites and malnutrition. Their standard daily diet consisted of *rotis* (flat bread) with salt; they seldom ate fresh fruits and vegetables.

Prior to the large-scale commercialization of agriculture, which removed cultivation from the hands of local communities, women possessed extraordinary knowledge and expertise in bio-diversity, food self-sufficiency, and natural remedies for illness. We wanted to help enable women to regain this responsibility and to restore their role in growing nutritious and affordable vegetables. We also wanted to improve women's health.

To help pursue our goals, ten local *gurdwaras* gave us rooms in which we could meet and land that we could cultivate. We created ten centers. Twenty-five women gathered daily in each one (about 250 women in all). They planted small organic vegetable gardens, in which they learned to grow a variety of seasonal crops, adding nutritious fresh vegetables and fruit to their families' diets. We organized workshops for them with faculty members from a nearby agricultural college on sustainable agriculture using organic seeds, fertilizers, and run off water from the *gurdwaras*.

Ghazala Khan with women in Sangrur

We organized free health camps that performed routine checkups and provided women with information about reproductive health, first aid, and home remedies for common illnesses. We also sponsored two screening camps for cataracts—a widespread problem in the region, and organized 100 cataract surgeries.

Building Bridges India, Sangrur

The women who attended our centers were keen to acquire skills that would enable them to earn incomes. To that end we organized vocational training for women in several handicraft industries. One of the most popular initiatives was the revival of *phulkari* (traditional Punjabi embroidery.) Women also produced garments and home wares. We hired a clothes designer from Delhi to offer women workshops on design and develop their entrepreneurial abilities. In addition to the material benefits that the centers provided, they created opportunities for women to develop camaraderie, share problems, and explore solutions to the challenges they faced.

If organic farming and income generating projects took off, some of my projects tanked. On a visit to Vermont, I met Jamie O'Shea, an idealistic young man who had ingeniously devised solar cookers. I invited him to Sangrur, and we travelled there from Delhi with two carloads crammed with equipment. Sadly, none of the five large solar cookers that Jamie built at the centers got much use. I attribute this in part to climate change. The sun barely broke through the clouds during the time he was in Sangrur and the cookers cracked when the monsoons hit. Jamie returned to his successful business, BjornQorn, producing solar cooked corn for upscale shops and restaurants in the US and the women of Sangrur continued using their woodburning stoves.

As gratifying as our work has been, I learned how difficult it is to bring about lasting and meaningful change. Creating an NGO in rural Punjab proved to be much harder than creating an NGO in the comfort of my home in Delhi. One problem involved overseeing the work from Delhi, which we partly resolved by having Ghazala spend half of each month in Sangrur. There were the practical difficulties that women faced in coming to the centers every day, given their domestic responsibilities and the poor quality of public transport. There was my own antipathy to facilitating sex-typed work, set against women's experience and interest in stitching and embroidery. I also had to reconcile my feminist

Building Bridges India, Sangrur

inclinations with the interest of many women to obtain training in order to create beauty parlors in the villages.

I still believed that film has a unique ability to capture the textured quality of people's lives. And I wanted to document the changes that have transpired in Sangrur in the five years since we had made *Harvest of Grief*. My dear friend, Deidi von Schawen, an acclaimed photographer, produced a powerful, half hour documentary entitled *Survivors of Sangrur*. Amrita, who translated and narrated the film, Deidi and I revisited families I knew and met others. We delved into the gendered dimensions of rural debt. We were struck by the extent to which family indebtedness was compounded by the high costs of the dowry, which not only impoverished families but also contributed to daughters' guilt, despite the fact that the young women we interviewed wanted to postpone marriages and find careers. The clarity with which these young women spoke was as inspiring as the obstacles in their way were daunting.

twelve

REFLECTIONS AND REMINISCENCES

As much as I've made homes in many places, I hate departures and separations. Each year, as I pack up to leave Delhi for New York—and vice versa—a part of me dies. I envy people who have always lived in the company of family and friends in just one place. From Chakalaka to Delhi, Monghyr, Tripoli, Cairo, Bangkok, and New York, with many places in between, I have made and left homes in so many places.

With Romen in our NY apartment

Painting of my house by Mary Helen Grace

My fear of separations has intensified amidst the losses of beloved family members, especially Maaji, Mamaji, Papaji, Patwant, Romen, my son-in-law Rob and, most recently, Mark's sister Judy. Leaving the places we've shared, feels like a more permanent separation from them than I'm willing to accept.

And yet each departure brings with it the anticipation of being with people and places I love. Although my daughters keep asking me to live with them year-round in the States, my soul is in India. Sitting in the garden of my home at Amrita Sher-Gil Marg, watching the bright green parrots perched on our tall trees and the ibis pecking seeds on the lawn takes me back to my childhood days and gives me a deep sense of tranquility and peace. But home is also in Des Moines where I probably have more friends than any other place in the world and I've been showered with hospitality by many friends who have visited me in India.

With Mary Helen Grace in Des Moines

And home is the house that Amrita and Mark built in an old apple orchard in Amherst and their little cottage on a tidal river in Gloucester, both homes filled with lively conversation and moments of contemplation. Ultimately, home is where my friends and family live.

Amrita, me, and Rekha in Amherst

With Rekha in Annapolis

With Amrita in NY

With Rekha in Woodstock

Robyn Brentano, Amrita, Pamela Philipose, and me in Delhi

With Pat Jones in Delhi

With Julie Gammack and Carol Guensberg in Delhi

*Mala Sekhri, Tejpavan Singh Gandhok (my grandnephew), Meher,
Rekha, Amrita, Suman Gandhok (my niece), Philippa Vaughan, me,
Deidi von Schaewen, and N.P. Singh in Delhi*

*With Mark, Teà (Becca's daughter), Becca, and Sandy Spadavecchia
(her husband) in Gloucester*

My home has always also been my work. To this day, writing grant proposals for Building Bridges India, producing films on Sangrur and writing these memoirs gives my life a sense of purpose. Perhaps my sense of urgency is fueled by witnessing the inequalities that remain and indeed have intensified. If for some people, age is associated with resignation, I find myself more outraged than ever by pervasive indignities and injustices. If, as feminists say, the personal is political, the political is also deeply personal for me. What keeps me up at night is the lynching of Muslims who are accused of consuming beef and the forced separation of undocumented immigrant parents and children in the US. It seems inconceivable that we have not only failed to achieve the goals outlined in the Universal Declaration of Human Rights, CEDAW and even the 1975 World Plan of Action for Women, but that the world's oldest and largest democracies are violating these rights with impunity.

And yet I continue to uphold the ideals that inspired me in the 1930s and '40s when I first awoke to nationalism, feminism, and humanism. With each defeat come new opportunities to make a difference in this big little world.

appendices

ARTICLES BY RASIL BASU

The Rape of Afghanistan
The Asian Age
3rd December, 2001

An unexpected fall-out of the September 11 attacks on the World Trade Centre and the Pentagon was the sudden concern of the American and other governments with the plight of Afghan women.

America retaliated by declaring war on Afghanistan to bring down the Taliban regime, end terrorism, and to capture Osama dead or alive. A further justification, added by President Bush in his address to the UN General Assembly, was the Taliban's treatment of women. Laura Bush went further in her radio address to the nation, with the plight of Afghan women providing her an entree into political life.

She was unequivocal in demanding that Afghan women be involved in rebuilding democracy in Afghanistan. It has taken 13 years for America to recognize the problem even though it contributed handsomely to the suffering of Afghan women, as it was less concerned with their situation and more with its own geopolitical interests during the period of Soviet occupation of Afghanistan.

During the occupation, in fact, women made enormous strides: illiteracy declined from 98' to 75', and they were granted equal rights with men in civil law, and in the Constitution. This is not to say that there was complete gender equality. Unjust patriarchal relations still prevailed in the workplace and in the family with women occupying lower level sex-type jobs. But the strides they took in education and employment were very impressive.

I witnessed these gains first hand when the UNDP assigned me (1986-88) as senior advisor to the Afghan government for women's development because of my long career with the United Nations working for women's advancement. During this period, I had drafted the World Plan of Action for Women and the draft Program for the Women's Decade, 1975-85 adopted at Mexico City Conference (1975) and Copenhagen Conference (1980). In Kabul I saw great advances in women's education and employment. Women were in evidence in industry, factories, government offices, professions and the media. With large numbers of men killed or disabled, women shouldered the responsibility of both family and country. I met a woman who specialized in war medicine which dealt with trauma and reconstructive surgery for the war-wounded. This represented empowerment to her. Another woman was a road engineer. Roads represented freedom—an escape from the oppressive patriarchal structures.

But as far back as 1988 1 could see the early warning signals as well. Even before the first Soviet troop withdrawal, "shabanamas," or handbills, warned of reprisals against women who left their homes. Followers of Gulbuddin Hekmatyar started throwing acid on women who dared to venture into the streets of Kabul in trousers, or skirts, or short-sleeved shirts. Ironically, the US favored the three fundamentalist resistance groups of "freedom fighters' headed by Hekmatyar, Khalis and Rabbani over the more moderate mujahideen groups. Saudi Arabian and American arms and ammunition gave the fundamentalists a vital edge over the moderates. Even more tragic is the fact that this military hardware was used, according to Amnesty International, to target unarmed civilians, most of them women and children. But more about that later.

In the fall of 1988, I wrote an article for an op-ed piece which I submitted to The New York Times, The Washington Post, and Ms Magazine. I pointed out that ascendant fundamentalism in Afghanistan had struck its first blow at women's education and employment. Since the Najibullah regime, which was still in power, was anxious to accommodate the opposition under its National Reconciliation Policy, women's rights were made the first offering.

It was no coincidence that the backlash started in the Ministry of Islamic Affairs, which began dismissing women on the pretext of abolition of posts. A strict code of dress was also imposed—a scarf to cover the head, the traditional full sleeved long tunic, and pants. Lunch breaks, which enabled women to meet, discuss problems, and protest against unfair practices, were stopped. So was co-education, which existed till sixth grade. With acute scarcity of resources, it was obvious that girls' schools would receive low priority and standards would drop. I recommended a number of steps which the western world, especially the US, could take to protect women's rights. In their aid programs they could insist on the integration of women in development projects. Women's colleges, vocational institutes, and NGOs could provide fellowships to women to study abroad. My recommendations were buried. And the above publications also preferred not to publish my piece, obviously, because it went against the perceived interests of the US.

The events, which followed, were worse than the direst predictions. The overthrow of the Najibullah government in 1992 led to fighting among warring fundamentalist groups for territorial control. Massive artillery attacks killed and wounded thousands of civilians, especially women and children. Afghan women's rights were violated with impunity as the constitution was suspended by the mujahideen groups who seized power in Kabul. The ruling warlords ignored the legal system, dismantled the judicial structure, assumed judicial functions for themselves in several provinces, and for the Islamic clergy or local shuras (councils of elders) in others. Trials were arbitrary and punishments were barbaric like stoning to death and public lashings of everyone including women. Amnesty International's report for the period April 1992—February 1995 lists horrendous crimes against women.

Rape by armed guards of the various warring factions was condoned by their leaders; it was viewed as a way of intimidating vanquished populations, and of rewarding soldiers. Fear of rape drove women to suicide, and fathers to kill their daughters to spare them the degradation. Scores of women were abducted and detained, sexually abused, and sold into prostitution. Most girls were victimized and tortured—because they belonged to different religious and ethnic groups. In addition to physical abuse, women were stripped of their fundamental rights of association, freedom of speech, of employment, and movement. The Supreme Court of the Islamic State in 1994, issued an Ordinance on Women's Veil which decreed that women should wear a veil to cover the whole body, forbidding them to leave their homes "not because they are women but for fear of sedition." This in a nutshell is the past record of the groups that form the Northern Alliance. Their warlords looked upon women as spoils of war—the very same warlords, who are now strutting around Kabul, with the support of the so-called civilized Western world under US leadership.

In February 1995, the Taliban (students of religion), a strong and popular political force, took control of nine out of thirty provinces and ushered in a new era. The Taliban established its own interpretation of strict Islamic code of ordinances and conduct. The Ministry of Promotion of Virtue and Prevention of Vice, also known as the moral police, was established. Its edicts banned women from working, or going to school, and forced them to wear the head to toe burqa. It ordered people to paint their first-floor windows black so that passersby could not see the women inside. A Taliban representative speaking from the Attorney General's office in Kabul explained the edict to journalists: "The face of a woman is a source of corruption for men who are not related to them.'

The UN Special Rapporteur for Violence against Women, Radhika Coomaraswamy of Sri Lanka, reported "official widespread, systematic violations of human rights of women in the Taliban areas of Afghanistan.' In many rape cases, she added, women were punished publicly for adultery and beaten for violations of the ministry's edicts, and under Rabbani's government from 1992-1996, some of the worst outrages against women were committed.

One exception to women's employment was made in the case of opium poppy cultivation as it is a labor-intensive task which men refused to undertake. The report of the UN Drug Control Program quotes a woman: "Our major problem is that weeding poppy fields takes a lot of time. We have problems carrying the seeds to the field and often get sick while lancing and collecting poppy.' With all the odds against them, Afghan women showed amazing bravery and heroism while resisting successive oppressive regimes. They often paid for it with their lives.

Foremost in the struggle was the Revolutionary Association of Women of Afghanistan (RAWA) formed in 1977. RAWA organized women through successive regimes to resist their oppression, by non-violent methods. It organized underground schools and health facilities for girls and women, and support and succor for rape victims, even in the refugee camps in Peshawar and Quetta. RAWA's founder, Meena Kamal, continued to work despite being repeatedly threatened for her "anti-jihad activities', till her assassination in 1987 in her house in Quetta. Although she had informed the Pakistani authorities of threats to her life, she was not provided police protection.

More recently (1993), the Afghan Women's Council (AWC) was formed by a number of professional Afghan women doctors, teachers and university lecturers to provide schools and health clinics for Afghan children and women in Pakistan's camps.

Though they worked towards raising awareness of women's rights within the framework of Afghanistan's religious and cultural tradition they too were threatened by mujahideen groups.

The war in Afghanistan has come full circle. As of today, the Taliban seems defeated in all Afghan cities. Osama bin Laden has not been captured 'dead or alive' nor is the terrorist network destroyed. No estimates exist of the toll war has taken of the lives of civilian men, women and children, nor of those permanently disabled or seriously wounded. The Northern Alliance, which is a conglomerate of various opportunistic ethnic groups mostly Tajiks, Hazaras and Uzbeks minus the Pashtuns, will play an important role in the formation of the next government. Needless to add they are the same groups who were in power before the Taliban.

Their treatment of women is well documented. The most recent indicator of the Northern Alliance's intent is the ban imposed by Interior Minister Younis Qanooni on a women's freedom march in Kabul, planned by Soraya Parlika of the newly-formed Union of Women in Afghanistan, for November 28. The ban, according to Parlika, is said to be "for security, but that is just a pretext... they don't want women to improve." The UN Special Envoy Frances Vendrell has been holding meetings with the exclusively male Northern Alliance and other political leaders but not met with any Afghan women. Is this a precursor of things to come?

Many of the countries—so-called victors of this "war'—have their own agendas in Afghanistan, and their own ideas about a future Afghan government. India is in a unique position to take up this issue with the Northern Alliance with whom it is on good terms. But will it?

Is it at all interested in raising its voice on behalf of the scarred Afghan women? It is of the utmost importance that the UN sponsored talks in Bonn and elsewhere take up these issues with the seriousness they deserve. US Secretary of State Colin Powell has underlined the need to involve women in the planning and implementation of the new government and as beneficiaries. Now is the time for him to stand up and be counted. RAWA must be invited to participate in the talks, and the views of Afghan women implemented. Minimum humane standards as set out in the Geneva Conventions must be impressed on the future government. Women's human rights should be safeguarded in any new Constitution.

The Missing Sex

"India's Bermuda Triangle", as you might imagine, does not lie in the confluence of the Arabian Sea and the Bay of Bengal with the Indian Ocean. It lies according to some, in the Punjab-Haryana-Himachal Pradesh belt where girls vanish without a trace even before they are born.

India's female-male sex ratio has declined (from 971 in 1901 to 933 according to the 2001 estimates) compared to the statistical norm worldwide, which is 1,050 females for every 1,000 males. In 1991 two states had child sex ratios below 880. In 2002, there are five states and union territories in this category, viz. Punjab (793), Haryana (820), Chandigarh (845), Delhi (865) and Gujarat (878). What is surprising also is that more prosperous states like Karnataka with better socio-economic indicators have also shown a dip in the child sex ratio from 960 in 1991 to 949 in 2001.

The declining sex ratio has been a cause of serious concern to demographers, sociologists, women's groups and thinking individuals. What is behind this continued drop in the sex ratio? The roots of the problem lie undoubtedly in the deep-seated patriarchal attitudes and the inferior status accorded to women along with unequal rights, social customs and practices such as dowry that lead to a preference for sons and a low or no valuation of girls.

The problem has been aggravated by the easy access to ultrasound machines since

1980 when ultrasound clinics sprang up all over the country. According to C. M. Francis of NGO Community Health Cell, "villages might not have clean drinking water but they have an ultrasound machine". Enterprising doctors with a desire to get rich fast, invested in portable ultrasound equipment and took them into remote villages, blatantly advertising the new technology that could reveal the sex of the unbom. In case the fetus was female there was a doctor or a midwife readily available to abort it. Illegally of course.

Concerned with the continuing drop in the sex ratio and the pressure from various groups, the Pre-Natal Diagnostic Techniques (Regulations and Prevention of Misuse) (PNDT) Act (Sep 20,1994) hastily put together, was passed without a minimal scrutiny, banning the practice except:

- where the pregnant woman is above 35 years of age;
- has undergone two or more spontaneous abortions;
- has been exposed to potentially teratogenic agents or has a family history of mental retardation or physical deformities or genetic diseases including chromosomal and blood or sex-linked genetic disorders.

Every genetic counselling center, laboratory or clinic carrying out these diagnostic techniques is required to be registered under the Act. The result of this Act was that the practice went underground and the fee for ultrasound was raised by unscrupulous doctors from Rs. 150 (approximately $10) to Rs.1500 ($30) and more recently to Rs.3600 ($72) to compensate for their undertaking the risk of criminal prosecution.

In Punjab alone, there are some 1500 clinics, the first being set up in Amritsar in 1972. The situation is expected to get worse with more and improved ultrasound machines.

According to S.C. Srivastava, Policy Director of the Central Government's Health Ministry, "the law looks better on paper than in practice". Registration of clinics has been slow and there has not been a single prosecution despite official acknowledgement of widespread abuse. One reason is that abortion up to the 20th week of pregnancy is legal, even though sex selection is not. How then will you prove that an abortion is done for sex selection when no receipt is given nor any kind of a diagnosis by the ultrasonologist?

Faced with this situation, Sabu George, an activist from CEHAT (Centre for Enquiry into Health and Allied Themes) and MASUM (Mahila Sarvangeen Utkarsh Mandal) filed a PIL (Public Interest Litigation) in the Supreme Court in Feb 2000 to activate the Central and State governments for implementation of the Act. The PIL also demanded amendments to ensure that pre-conception and during conception selection techniques are not used. On 4th May the Supreme Court passed an order ensuring the implementation of the Act, plugging some of the loopholes but did not consider the second objective.

> What has been the impact of legal and judicial action? Before making any kind of an assessment it is necessary to take a closer look at some of the provisions of the Act.

> In a country where girls are married off in their teens, especially in rural areas and pregnancies occur shortly after, to set the minimum age for ultrasound at 35 seems quite absurd.

> The whole purpose of ultrasound is to detect if there are any abnormalities in the fetus or there is a danger to the mother's health.

In the words of Amartya Sen, the Nobel Prize winning economist (as quoted by Sudha Ramachandran in Development and Cooperation No. 1 Jan/Feb 2002), "It's a technological revolution of a reactionary kind". With due respects, I might add that the reactionary element comes in only in India and in other high son preference societies such as China and South Korea. In Western countries ultrasound has certainly proved its worth in cases of multiple fetuses, deformed babies, cranio-facial deformities, congenital disorders, malpositions, placenta previa where corrective measures could be taken in time. Innumerable perinatal deaths of pregnant women have been prevented by detecting "pregnancies at risk. "It is therefore obligatory for doctors in the West to do one or more ultrasounds. It is ironic that the same techniques which are used to save lives in the West are used in India to kill female fetuses. Ultrasound is a very safe, non-invasive and relatively cheap mode of investigation. It is much safer than alternate means for sex determination such as amniocentesis, chorionic biopsy, chromosomal studies, etc.

Laws are only as good as their enforcement. As this law is a first, it is only by enforcing it that flaws and loopholes can be identified. If violators can get away with impunity by paying bribes under the table, it makes a mockery of the law. At the same time there are genuine cases of hospitals and centers getting prosecuted or harassed by "appropriate authorities" for some or no irregularity under the law. That the law needs some essential amendments is clear.

An ordinance presented by the Union Cabinet to amend the Act awaits the sanction of the President. The amendment leaves intact the provision restricting the age of eligibility for ultrasound to 35 years of age. Addressing a press conference, Dr. Gupta, president of the Delhi Medical Association said, "A curb on ultrasound in order to prevent sex determination tests would deprive women of their basic right to be diagnosed and treated for a number of ailments both in pre-conception stage and post conception stage". He said further, "...most Indian women plan their families in their twenties and in case there is a complication the doctor will be in a dilemma whether to conduct an ultrasound or not". Dr. Gupta, supported by the Indian Medical Association of over one lakh doctors, has threatened to file a public interest litigation against the amendment.

Another controversial provision is the one whereby a pregnant woman can get a test done by getting the consent of the Central Supervisory Board which is to be set up under the Act. The doctors of the DMA stated that in case of an emergency it is most unpractical for a patient or a doctor to go to the Board for permission (Asian Age, 4 June 2002).

The anomaly that exists between the provisions of the Medical Termination of Pregnancy (MTP) Act and the PNDT Act needs to be removed. But the single most important thing is to raise public awareness about women's rights and to enhance the valuation attached to the girl child. Says Dr. Mira Shiva of the Voluntary Health Association of India, "Daughters are seen as an expense particularly because of the dowries families pay to marry them off. Under such circumstances, the law banning sex selection is a non-starter".

A most puzzling result of the increasing shortage of girls according to Sabu George is, much greater violence against surviving women. Social workers claim there are more rapes and harassment in communities where boys greatly outnumber girls. Strange that girls don't even acquire a scarcity value.

Women in Shreds

According to the Vedas, violence which brutalizes people, assumes three forms: those who commit violence or have it committed, those who suffer violence, and those who remain silent witnesses. How ironic, that the proponents of Hindutva—born of a peaceful faith should be the advocates and perpetrators of violence against Muslims in Gujarat, a minority community, irrespective of gender and age. This article however deals with the bestiality of crimes against women in a country which claims- at least- to hold women in high esteem.

Stories of violent sexual crimes against women are surfacing from the testimonies of survivors, the reports of human rights groups, and newspaper and television reporters. Every woman's story tells a horrific tale of torture, rape and burning. The unprecedented scale of savagery that preceded and followed rape is mind-blowing.

In a Public Hearing of the Gujarat Genocide Survivors in Delhi on 26 April, organized by Communalism Combat and Sahmat, around 40 victims narrated outrageous incidents in which whole families were sadistically wiped out with the exception of one or two survivors who managed to escape. The police on some pretext or the other, did not entertain their FIRS especially since direct evidence of the rape and killings was often destroyed through the extermination of most of the eyewitnesses with the exception of very young children. But the reports, which have come from organizations or groups that have visited Gujarat, corroborate the information from victims.

"I have never known a riot which has used the sexual subjugation of women so widely as an instrument of violence as in the recent mass barbarity in Gujarat. There are reports everywhere of gang rape, of young girls and women, often in the presence of members of their families, followed by their murder by burning them alive, or by bludgeoning them with a hammer and in one case with a screw driver." (Report of the Citizen's Initiative titled, 'The Survivors Speak') "Among the women surviving in relief camps are many who have suffered the most bestial forms of sexual violence including mass rape, stripping, insertion of objects into their body and molestations. A majority of rape victims have been burnt alive." (April 16, 2002)

Even pregnant women were not spared these atrocities. Their bellies were cut open and the fetus pulled out before their eyes before being killed. A gravedigger told Human Rights Watch woman who washed the bodies of female victims before burial at the same site told Human Rights Watch, the same organization that "I washed the bodies of female victims before burial. Some bodies had heads missing, some had hands missing, and some were like coal, when you touched them they would crumble. Some women's bodies had been split down the middle."

Quite a few of the worst instances of violence against women and young girls took place in Naroda Patia. One woman from Naroda says, "some girls even threw themselves into the fire, so as not to get raped." A ten-year old girl added, "l saw it also, they cut them down in the middle." In another case a nine-year-old girl interviewed said, "Main bataoon Didi, Balatkaar ka matlab-jab aurat ko nanga kahe hain aur phir useyjala detay hain" (Rape is when a woman is stripped naked and then burnt). The same pattern was repeated over and over again in Vadodra, Ahmedabad and surrounding areas. The Human Rights Watch Report states that members of Bajrang Dal and VHP were preparing for these attacks by distributing arms in rural areas as far back as six months before the communal violence began.

The AIDWA (All India Democratic Women's Association) and the CPI (M) representatives first-hand accounts provide a grim picture of the worst state sponsored carnage against the Muslim community. The numbers of women and children attacked and burnt were far greater than the official figures. According to government estimates there are about one lakh people in relief camps—even though there is no such thing as relief. The dismal conditions in the overcrowded camps with no clothes, food, toilet facilities and very little water have led to all kinds of illnesses and mental trauma. There is now talk of closing even these camps with no thought given to where those ousted will go? In the absence of FIRS there is no question of compensation as there is no registration of killings, added to which is the horror Muslims face of seeing their homes, properties, businesses and vehicles destroyed as part of a systematic plan to eliminate their assets and render them powerless.

Now let us turn to the government's response. In the Lok Sabha debate on violence in Gujarat, George Fernandes said, what is new about rape, all this hue and cry that is being raised by relating such stories is as if for the first time a mother has been killed and her fetus taken out, or where a daughter has been raped before her mother's eyes? Has all this happened for the first time? Did this not happen in 1984?"

What is new about these rapes was very poignantly described by George Fernandes, "Every woman is new about rape...Every scream is new about rape... Every death is new about rape... Every child who smelt burnt flesh is new about rape. "What is also new about rape, says George Fernandes, is that this savage crime has been only resorted to in situations of armed conflict, civil war, foreign occupation, or insurgency. It is new when a democratically elected government uses its party, in this case, its Sangh Parivar, its police, and its administrators to rape and plunder and kill its own people. Tragically the only exception to this rule was also in India in 1984 when violence, brutality, burning and killing of Sikhs was undertaken by the ruling party with the support of political leaders and the police and state apparatus. Are we to understand that since it happened before, it has acquired legitimacy? And the state machinery is justified in inciting violence and supplying official lists of electoral rolls, and detailed lists of minority-owned businesses, buildings, homes and vehicles to facilitate the task of eliminating them? It appears so, judging from Mr. Advani the Home Minister's statement, in the Lok Sabha, "I, responsible for law and order in India defend the killing of thousands under Gujarat's BJP regime because you, the Congress let 3.000 Sikhs be killed in Delhi 18 years ago." In Gujarat the Sangh Parivar went a step further and organized armed militias to do its bidding. In a confidential report to KPS Gill, the newly appointed security adviser, the Gujarat police has stated that the state's political leaders "subverted" the police reducing them to a "pliant and subservient force".

As to the moral culpability of those who facilitated criminal acts let us look at some of our women politicians holding positions of political power. To start with Mayawati and her unprincipled politics. No sooner had she taken over as Chief Minister of UP, she shut her eyes and ears to the screams of the women and child victims saying, "those who were behind the killings of the *karsewaks* at Godhra were behind the riots that took place elsewhere in Gujarat."

Jayalalitha, the Chief Minister of Tamil Nadu took the high moral ground that it was not morally correct for the Chief Minister of one state to criticize the Chief Minister of another. This at a time when there was a hue and cry by women's organizations and others to dismiss Narendra Modi the perpetrator of the Gujarat riots. Mamata Banerjee, the leader of the Trinamul Congress, despite her earlier statements against Modi did not vote for his ouster. The record of women members of the state assembly is no better.

As for the National Commission for Women its members did not even visit Gujarat until five weeks after the carnage began. (9th April). The report of the Commission in contrast to the findings of the National Human Rights Commission and the National Commission for Minorities describes the carnage against the Muslims as "communal disturbances" turning its back on the savagery against Muslim women. It absolves the state government of responsibility and does not care to identify the perpetrators of violence. What kind of a Commission for Women is this? Is it just one more institution appropriated by the BJP and its Sangh Parivar to carry out its agenda?

The long-term damage to the nation of the massacres is not hard to imagine. The survivors of the Gujarat holocaust who lost their mothers and fathers or siblings, have been completely brutalized and scarred for life. The complicity of the State and the Central Government in the genocide against the Muslims is evident from the dismissal of the carnage by Narendra Modi as "the natural and justifiable anger of the people" and the Prime Minister's defense that the problem was caused by the "trouble making Muslims."

The violence and the killings continue. No steps have been taken to stop them. Narendra Modi is still the Chief Minister with the support of the Central Government and the perpetrators of the crimes have neither been tried nor their barbarities curtailed. India that was once at the vanguard for the rights of the oppressed people in South Africa and the Palestinians now stands guilty of the most serious crimes against humanity. Violating the norms of international humanitarian law and the Geneva Conventions, India stands condemned in the court of world public opinion.

Rasil Basu, Chairperson Ekatra, 21 May 2002

Afghanistan Revisited

The Sept. 11 observances and President Donald Trump's speech last month have returned Afghanistan to the headlines. The president said a rapid exit of U.S. forces, there since after the terror attacks of 2001, would leave a void that terrorist groups would fill.

I listened with an equal sense of irony and foreboding, as he called on India and Pakistan to step in and help rout the Taliban and other such groups out of Afghanistan.

If past is precedent, that could be at worst a dangerous, and at best an unviable prospect. As a United Nations Development Program consultant, I lived in Afghanistan's capital city of Kabul in the late 1980s advising the Soviet-backed government at the time on elevating the role of women. From that vantage point, I was witness to the early rise of the Taliban before it grew into one of the greatest repressors of women the world has known and destroyed the progress we had helped to make.

I also recall the United States' contributions to its inception and growth. The sad truth is, had it not been for U.S. administrations in the 1980s and '90s arming and funding some of the Taliban's radical Islamist precursors, Afghanistan may not have turned into what Trump calls "a government that gave comfort and shelter to terrorists."

"The Americans hoped that the Taliban could bring peace and stability to Afghanistan," wrote former Pakistani President Pervez Musharraf in his 2006 book, In the Line of Fire. He wrote the U.S. "welcomed the emergence of a 'third force'..." but later dissociated themselves from the Taliban.

Though Trump is not to blame for that history, there were other, more moderate wings of the Mujahedeen the United States could have supported, which shared the American objective of getting the Soviets out. But U.S. policy favored the political Islamists, joining Saudi Arabia in supporting them with arms and ammunition. Those would be used against the moderates favored by Afghanistan's then Minister of Defense Ahmad Shah Massoud, who was appointed in 1992 in post-communist Afghanistan

Massoud expressed grave concerns about the Taliban, which originated out of religious schools for Afghan refugees in Pakistan. He particularly objected to their repression of Afghan women. In 1994-95 he helped defeat most militant factions in Kabul but with massive military support from Pakistan, the Taliban regrouped and expanded from their base in Kandahar to the capital to emerge as a new militant fundamentalist force. Massoud was killed two days before Sept. 11, 2001 in a suicide bombing.

Trump now calls for Pakistani assistance to rid Afghanistan of such groups. How likely is that when Pakistan has historically done the opposite? In the 1990s, the head of Pakistan's Inter-Services Intelligence (ISI), Hamid Gul, wanted Pakistan's mujahedeen to establish a government in Afghanistan for an Islamic revolution that would spread to Central Asia. According to Pakistani journalist Ahmed Rashid 80,000 to 100,000 Pakistanis fought for the Taliban in Afghanistan. Pakistan's ISI was also actively involved with several Al-Qaeda training camps in 2000, according to British intelligence.

Two years after the Taliban seized Kabul in 1996 to establish the Islamic Emirate of Afghanistan, a U.S. State Department document said between 20 percent and 40 percent of Taliban soldiers were Pakistani.

In 2000, the U.N. Security Council imposed an arms embargo against military support to the Taliban, with a notable focus on Pakistan. By 2001, 28,000 to 30,000 Pakistani nationals were reportedly fighting anti-Taliban forces in Afghanistan.

"We have been paying Pakistan billions and billions of dollars, at the same time they are housing the very terrorists that we are fighting," said Trump. He said 20 U.S.-designated foreign terrorist organizations are active in Afghanistan and Pakistan.

"The terrorist of yesterday is the hero of today, and the hero of yesterday becomes the terrorist of today," wrote Pakistani author and political scientist Eqbal Ahmed in his 2011 book, Terrorism: Theirs and Ours. He recalled that President Ronald Reagan in 1985 hosted Afghan mujahedeen and called them "freedom fighters."

As for India, Trump has noted its contributions to stability in Afghanistan, but suggested its U.S. trade could be jeopardized unless India steps up its Afghan involvement. Yet even as he bases his Afghan strategy on co-operation from India and Pakistan, the president acknowledged they are, "two nuclear-armed states, whose tense relations threaten to spiral into conflict." That could certainly result if they get involved on opposite sides.

It is doubtful that creating a viable democratic Afghanistan is something the U.S. can achieve. Afghanistan was never a cohesive, centrally planned state. It was a nomadic, tribal Islamic society held together by village settlements. Even the Soviet hold was at best tenuous in the cities and extended to only 20 percent of the countryside. The USSR couldn't hold onto Afghanistan; nor could the U.S. win the war.

As an Indian woman who has worked over 60 years toward global women's empowerment in New York, Afghanistan and India, and currently lives under the Hindu-centric government of India's Prime Minister Narendra Modi, I see both the perils of militant Islamic fundamentalism and of the growing global anti-Muslim sentiment. To be blunt: Accelerating the existing tensions between those two South Asian nations and intensifying the tenuous status of Muslims targeted under Modi's regime could create a very dangerous, if not critical, situation in the region.

Rasil Basu was in Kabul from the spring of 1986 through the summer of 1988 as the Senior UNDP Advisor to the Afghan Government for Integrating Women in the Planning Process. She can be reached at rasilsinghbasu@gmail.com.

COLUMNS BY REKHA BASU

Fond memories: Rekha Basu and her mother, Basil Basu, in the kitchen, at left, and on Rekha's wedding day.

How a magazine helped one family adapt to America

REKHA BASU

Last week, Des Moines-based Meredith Corp. announced it was buying four more magazines. All are reputable and have their followings. All — Parents, Fitness, Child and Family Circle — are good sources.

But one in particular awoke decades-old memories for me. Because it played a pivotal role in my childhood, it seems appropriate for it to be making Des Moines its home, just as I have.

Family Circle can be credited with helping my Indian-born mother adapt to an American way of life. This wasn't the sort of magazine you'd expect to find on my parents' Manhattan coffee table, between the New York Times and journals about art, economics and foreign affairs.

But it was usually there.

My mother, who had gotten a law degree at Yale and worked in the human rights division of the United Nations, could, and still can, converse with anyone on just about anything. She knew good food and entertained with style. But what she wasn't prepared for was being a working parent in America and having to feed a family every night.

Middle-class families in India employ others to do the cooking. And Indian food is painstakingly prepared — full of chopping and grinding and overnight soaking. Now there are shortcuts on the market, but back then you couldn't just come home at the end of the day and whip up an Indian meal.

So the lamb vindaloo and biryani were reserved for when there was more time to cook and when my sister and I were old enough to help. With the help of Family Circle and Woman's Day, my mother learned the magic of pairing cream of mushroom soup with frozen green beans. She learned about adding dehydrated onion soup mix to ground beef to make meat loaf, and about using canned fish to make tuna casseroles. And she learned about instant puddings and jello with canned fruit.

OK, those recipes, with all the canned and frozen stuff, had a high kitsch factor. Some of it was bland and boring. On weekends, there was time for fancier fare, and my father often turned out gourmet international meals. But for the work week, my mother's salvation came in the magazine's weekly menu planner.

There was something oddly reassuring about the sight of her reading her Family Circle with her feet up after dinner. In the fast-paced life we lived, it was wholesome and comforting, like a pot of soup bubbling on the stove. It was a bit of Middle America for a non-American family in a New York City high-rise.

So I'd nestle beside her and read it, too. I'd read the heartwarming true-life stories and the helpful household hints on removing stains and stretching the life of flowers. In an uncertain world — the Vietnam War, racial apartheid — the magazine suggested there was no problem so severe it couldn't be solved with a cup of hot cocoa and some fresh-baked cookies.

Long before Martha Stewart lent her designer imprint to the domestic arts, Family Circle brought a no-frills approach to feeding a family and making a home. It said it was OK to be less than a perfectionist about doing everything from scratch. Woman's Day did much the same thing, but Family Circle tried, at least in its name, to be gender-neutral.

Sadly, our society has often pitted stay-at-home mothers against working ones. It's created the myth that sewing and cooking and taking care of kids are the exclusive province of the full-time homemaker, and that working mothers look down on the stuff of homemakers do.

But my mother embraced all of it. Though she'd had clothes tailor-made in India, she also learned to make dresses for my sister and me using patterns. She knitted, crocheted and gardened.

I haven't cracked a Family Circle in years. Grocery-store shelves are cluttered with specialized lifestyle magazines now. Some teach you how to live as a vegetarian and some teach an expensive way to lead a simpler life. Some focus on how to raise children and some on how to be physically fit. Each has its market because reading them is about more than getting advice. It's about belonging to a certain group and sharing an identity with the others in it.

Family Circle has given millions of people guilt-free ideas to heat back on time spent in the kitchen. Reading it doesn't put you in the Martha Stewart or Oprah Winfrey clubs. You probably wouldn't boast of having gotten a recipe from it.

But in this multi-tasking world, it's taught folks how to make pigs in blankets from frozen hot dogs and croissant dough, and pizzas from English muffins.

The purists among us might scoff at those lessons. But over-extended parents still recognize their value. I still use some of the recipes.

REKHA BASU can be reached at rbasu@dmreg.com or (515) 284-8584.

IOWA LIFE

SALUTING MOTHERS

I could never be all that she is, but she has taught me to be OK with what I am.

When I was around 15, and at a dinner party with my parents, a guest took my face in his hand and scrutinized it. "Let's see," he said. "Will you ever have your mother's beauty?" Dropping his hand, he shook his head and answered his own question with a firm, "No."

REKHA BASU
rbasu@dmreg.com

What the man lacked in tact he made up for in taste. It was true. Even some of my high school crushes found my mother beautiful. As Rasil Basu's daughter, you got used to hearing how exceptional your mother was in this or that way that you could never measure up to. She'd graduated from high school in India in her early teens, completed college, resisting the arranged marriages her peers were succumbing to, and won a fellowship to Yale Law School, becoming one of the first women ever to attend. She joined the United Nations human rights division in New York and helped set its priorities for women's rights.

She also knitted our sweaters, sewed our dresses, gardened and cooked — and in her younger days, played tennis and badminton with her sari hitched up.

I was not my mother's daughter. I was the last to be picked on a sports team, and was a mediocre, undisciplined student, more interested in hanging out and going to protest marches than following the model of achievement the other

See BASU, Page 4E

Register columnist Rekha Basu's mother, Rasil Basu, in a photo from the 1990s.
SPECIAL TO THE REGISTER

Rekha Basu and her mother, Rasil, in 2010. SPECIAL TO THE REGISTER

'MAYBE I AM MY MOTHER'S DAUGHTER, AFTER ALL'

BASU

Continued from Page 1E

Asian kids around us had to live up to.

But my mother was laid back about it. She seemed to have faith that once I felt passionate enough about something to really work at it, I'd be OK.

More important, she loved me the way I was. She may not have kept a baby book, or dropped me off at college and made the dorm bed, as I did for my sons. But she wrote excuses to get me out of gym class so we could eat lunch together, where we would giggle and have fun. She was open to trying anything. She exposed my sister and me to everything from high art to experimental "encounter group" theater.

Much later, when I had teenage sons and she was visiting, I once walked into the family room and saw they had her watching a vulgar South Park movie. Embarrassed, I insisted they shut it. The next day, my mother asked when they could finish watching it.

My mother has always had passionate values about equality and justice which

she has modeled in a real-life acceptance of anyone. Everyone could be her friend, no matter their beliefs, political affiliation or social standing.

When I was growing up, she was the pillar of support for a succession of widowed or divorced women who might call the house drunk and crying and she'd comfort them. At my parents' 50th anniversary, my younger son toasted that his grandparents "came to Des Moines and stole all our friends." More accurately, from the woman conducting an estate sale we went to, to my sons' elementary art teacher, my mother turned casual acquaintances into dear friends. Some have since visited her in India.

So has Pastor John Palmer of the Des Moines First Assembly of God Church, with a group of fellow ministers. In her living room, they formed a circle, bowed heads and prayed to Jesus — my Sikh mother right along with them. I took her with me to visit Indian Prince Manvendra, the world's first openly gay member of royalty, whose own mother had tried to disinherit him. By the end of our stay, my mother and he had adopted each other.

When I was around 11, I

spent a weekend on a school field trip at a camp. When the other girls shared intimacies at night, I talked about my closeness to my mother. The counselor was disapproving, telling me that was an unhealthy attachment, and I needed to separate. I know I can't hold onto her forever. But what I get from her in her lifetime will help to carry me through my own.

A dear friend recently paid me a compliment that compensates for those superficial digs from my childhood. She called me one of the most resilient people she knows. I have no doubt about where I got that. But I also know not everyone has been nurtured that way. Some people I greatly admire have found resilience by having to fend for themselves.

As I've aged, I have come to realize that it wasn't the qualities in my mother I could never have that were most decisive for me. It's the ones anyone could have: Learning to accept and enjoy people for who they are; having fun and embracing life to its fullest; and loving those close to you as hard as you can.

Maybe I am my mother's daughter, after all.

Made in the USA
Middletown, DE
30 March 2019